MASTERING ASCENSION

KEYS TO THE KINGDOM SERIES
POCKET EDITION

THIS BOOK SHOULD NOT BE LEFT ACCESSIBLE, IN CLEAR VIEW, OR SHARED CASUALLY WITH OTHERS

Published from
Mardukite Borsippa HQ, San Luis Valley, Colorado
Mardukite Academy & Systemology Society
for spiritual or philosophical purposes only

MASTERING ASCENSION

Systemology
Advanced Training Course
Manual #7

As presented by Joshua Free
to the Systemology Society

THE JOSHUA FREE IMPRINT
JFI PUBLICATIONS

ISBN : 978-1-961509-54-2

This manual is restricted to students on
The Systemology Advanced Training Course
that have already completed the
"Pathway to Ascension" Professional Course

References to prerequisite material:
Processing-Levels 0 to 6 (PC-1 to 16)
"The Secret of Universes" (AT #1)
"Games, Goals & Purposes" (AT #2)
"The Jewel of Knowledge" (AT #3)
"Implanted Universes" (AT #4)
"Entities & Fragments" (AT #5)
"Spiritual Perception" (AT #6)

Full use of this manual may also require:
"Systemology Biofeedback"
"Systemology Procedures" and
"Systemology Piloting"

First Edition Pocket Paperback — *April 2024*

mardukite.com

The Keys to the Kingdom are Yours for the Taking!

The official Mardukite Systemology "Advanced Training Course" is now available in print for the first time.

Those Seekers that have completed the "Pathway to Ascension" Systemology Professional Course can now access the upper-level teachings of our tradition.

This book is not for everyone...
This is the third manual for Level-8.

Never before has Joshua Free presented this material outside the confines of the Mardukite NexGen Systemology Society.

Learn how to expertly apply our spiritual technology toward reaching higher levels of Awareness and Beingness than ever before thought possible for humanity on planet Earth.

Each of the "Keys to the Kingdom" Advanced Training Course Manuals will further a Seekers reach on the Pathway leading out of this Universe.

<u>The Pathway to Ascension Professional Course</u>

#1 – *Increasing Awareness (Level-0)*
#2 – *Thought & Emotion (Level-0)*
#3 – *Clear Communication (Level-0)*
#4 – *Handling Humanity (Level-1)*
#5 – *Free Your Spirit (Level-2)*
#6 – *Escaping Spirit-Traps (Level-2)*
#7 – *Eliminating Barriers (Level-3)*
#8 – *Conquest of Illusion (Level-3)*
#9 – *Confronting the Past (Level-4)*
#10 – *Lifting the Veils (Level-4)*
#11 – *Spiritual Implants (Level-5)*
#12 – *Games and Universes (Level-5)*
#13 – *Spiritual Energy (Level-6)*
#14 – *Spiritual Machinery (Level-6)*
#15 – *The Arcs of Infinity (Level-6)*
#16 – *Alpha Thought (Level-6)*

<u>Keys to the Kingdom Advanced Training</u>

#1 – *The Secret of Universes (Level-7)*
#2 – *Games, Goals & Purposes (Level-7)*
#3 – *The Jewel of Knowledge (Level-7)*
#4 – *Implanted Universes (Level-7)*
#5 – *Entities & Fragments (Level-8)*
#6 – *Spiritual Perception (Level-8)*
#7 – *Mastering Ascension (Level-8)*
#8 – *Advancing Systemology (Level-8)*

Systemology Biofeedback
Systemology Procedures
Systemology Piloting

TABLET OF CONTENTS

Advanced Manuals should be studied in the sequential order in which they are numbered.

INTRODUCTION TO THE MANUAL

This manual is restricted to students on
The Systemology Advanced Training Course
that have already completed the
"Pathway to Ascension" Professional Course

References to prerequisite material:
Processing-Levels 0 to 6 (PC-1 to 16)
"The Secret of Universes" (AT #1)
"Games, Goals & Purposes" (AT #2)
"The Jewel of Knowledge" (AT #3)
"Implanted Universes" (AT #4)
"Entities & Fragments" (AT #5)
"Spiritual Perception" (AT #6)

Full use of this manual may also require:
"Systemology Biofeedback"
"Systemology Procedures" and
"Systemology Piloting"

THE SYSTEMOLOGY ADVANCED TRAINING COURSE MANUAL SERIES

Mardukite Systemology is a new evolution in Human understanding about the "systems" governing *Life, Reality,* the *Universe* and all *Existences.* It is also a *Spiritual Path* used to transcend the Human experience and reach *"Ascension."*

This is an *Advanced Training* (*AT*) course manual detailing *upper-levels* of our spiritual philosophy. It is intended to assist *advancing* a *Seeker's* personal progress toward the *upper-most levels* of the *Pathway.*

This manual follows after our *Professional Course* series of lessons—available as individual booklets, or collected in two volumes titled *"The Pathway to Ascension"* The *Professional Course* follows after material given in the *Basic Course* booklets, or *"Fundamentals of Systemology"* volume.

The systematic methodology that we use to assist an individual to increase their *"Actualized Awareness"* (and reach gradually higher toward their *"Spiritual Ascension"*) is referred to as *"The Pathway"*—and that individual is called a *"Seeker."*

To receive the greatest benefit from this manual: it is expected that a *Seeker* will already be familiar with the fundamental concepts and terminology (previously relayed in the *Basic Course* and *Professional Course* lessons) of our *applied philosophy*.

As a *Seeker* increases their *Awareness* in this lifetime, their spiritual *"Knowingness"* also increases—which is to say their *certainty* on *Life*, on this and other *Universes*, and on *realizing Self* as an unlimited "spiritual being" *having* an enforced restrictive "human experience." A *Seeker* also *knowingly* increases their command and control of the "human experience." And this is a part of what is meant by *"Actualized Awareness."*

CHARTING FLIGHTS ON THE PATHWAY

Although there is a systematic structure to *fragmentation,* the personal journey experienced along the *Pathway* will be different for each *Seeker.* For example, certain areas will seem more *"turbulent"* or difficult for one *Seeker* than another. We tend to say that these areas have more *"charge"* on them—or that they are more *"heavily charged."* It is best to handle such areas when you are already feeling "good" and not in a situation (or condition) where that specific area is consistently being *"triggered"* or *"restimulated."*

As an applied philosophy, *Systemology* "theory" can be easily utilized in the "laboratory" of the "world-at-large" in everyday life. This is implied within the basic instruction of each lesson. Unlike other "sciences" that conduct experiments by making a change to some "objective variable" *out there* and waiting to see an effect, our focus is the individual (or *Observer*) themselves, and how *they* affect the *"Reality"* perceived.

Our philosophy is applied by using specific exercises and systematic techniques. These *"processes"* provide the most stable personal gain (and *realizations*) for each area; but only when actually applied with a *Seeker's* full *"presence"* and *Awareness.* Hundreds of such *processes* may be found in the *"Pathway to Ascension"* (*Professional Course*) material.

Applying a technique is called *"running a process." Processes* are designed with very simple instructions or *"command-lines."* To *run* a *processing command-line,* a *Seeker* may be assisted by the communication of that *line* from a *"Co-Pilot"* (as in *"Traditional Piloting"*). But even then, a *Seeker* must still personally "input" the *command* as *Self.* For this reason—and quite thankfully—*Solo-Processing* is possible.

Processing Techniques are intended to treat the *Spiritual Being* or *Alpha-Spirit*; the individual themselves. The *"command-lines"* are *directed to* the individual themselves—not some *mental machinery* of theirs, and not even a *Biofeedback* metering device.

Systematic Processing is applied by the *Alpha-Spirit*—who then *Self-directs* command of their "Mind-System" or "body" (*genetic-vehicle*), both of which are "constructs" that the *Alpha-Spirit* (*Self*, or the "I-AM" *Awareness unit*) operates, but neither of which is actually *Self*. *Fragmentation* causes *Humans* to falsely identify *Self as* the *"Mind"* or even a *"Body."*

Some *processes* can be treated quite lightly at first; others may require a bit of working at in order to get *"running"* well. It is important to set aside a period of time when you can be dedicated to your studies and *processing*. This period of time is referred to as a "*processing session.*" When a *process* does start *running* well, it is important to be able to complete it to a satisfactory "*end-point.*"

Processing allows us to be able to *actually* "look" at *things* and even determine the *considerations* we have made—or attitudes we have decided—about *Reality* as a result of those experiences.

It doesn't do us much good to simply "glance"—or to *restimulate* something uncomfortable and then quickly *withdraw* from it once again, leaving more of our *attention* yet again behind and held fixedly on it.

Generally speaking, a *Seeker* continues to *run* a *process* so long as something is "happening"—which is to say, the *process* is still producing a change. Usually this is evident by the type of "answers" that a *command-line* prompts a *Seeker* to originate from the database of their own *Mind-System.*

Processing Command-Lines ("PCL") are not "magic words"; they do not "do" anything on their own. They systematically assist a *Seeker* to direct their own attention toward increasing *Awareness.*

A *Seeker* may also cease to generate new "data" from a *process* without reaching an *"ultimate" realization* as an *"end-point."* It is possible that additional "layers" (or even other "areas") require handling before anything "deeper" is accessible. If this is the case, end the *process.* But, if a *Seeker* is *withdrawing* from something uncomfortable that was incited or stirred up, then a *process* is *run* until they feel "good" about it.

One of the benefits to *Flying-Solo* on the *Pathway* is that the *processing* is entirely *Self-determined.* This naturally provides a certain built-in "safety" for a practitioner. Anything you *restimulate* by *Self-determinism* is *your thing.* It is not triggered or incited by some external *"other-determined"* influences (or other "source-points") that make you an *effect.* It can be more easily handled in *processing*—or you can simply let things "cool down" and come back to it again in another *session.*

While it may seem "mysterious" to beginners, a *Seeker* gets a sense for knowing how long to *run* a *process* only with practice. Once you have spent some time actually applying material from *"The Pathway to Ascension" Professional Course,* there are many aspects of it that become "second nature" because they are, in fact, a part of our true original native nature. All we have done in *Systemology* is *"reverse engineer"* the routes of *creation* and *consideration* that are already *our own.*

SYSTEMOLOGY LEVEL-8

We are publishing *"upper-level" Systemology* in *2024* for the very first time. Its effective application is dependent on a *Seeker* having already reached a stable point of *"Beta-Defragmentation."* This requires proper use of materials for *processing-levels 0 to 6*—as given in the *"Pathway to Ascension" Professional Course* (available in two volumes, or sixteen individual booklets).

Additionally, this current *Systemology Level-8* work is a direct continuation of *Level-7*, which *must* be completed before continuing. The *Systemology Level-7* manuals—*"The Secret of Universes," "Games, Goals & Purposes," "The Jewel of Knowledge"* and (to a lesser extent) *"Implanted Universes"*—should be treated as a single "unit" of work *prior* to approaching *Level-8*. These manuals are available individually, or as collected in *Volume One* of the *"Keys to the Kingdom" Advanced Training (A.T.) Course.*

After uncovering *"The Jewel"* and discovering the "secret" of *Universes*, a *"Seeker"* has *found* the "hidden gem" of the *Pathway* at *Level-7*, and is no longer a *"Seeker."* Of course, things are not always what we expect—and *"all that glitters is not gold."* Yet, still, it is *"The Jewel of Knowledge"* (*Parts #1-5*) and the *Entry-Point Heaven Incident, &tc.*, that represents the "ceiling" of *this Universe* and even what is behind it, beneath it, or embedded into its structure. It was what a *"Seeker"* had been *drawn* to in their *search*, but was never meant to find by any other method or avenue, except *systematically*.

Systemology Level-8 is the first official *"Wizard Level"* of the *Systemology Society*. As stated in *A.T. Manual #4*: while "formal" *Advanced Training* may end with manuals representing *Systemology Level-8* (and completing the *"Keys to the Kingdom"* series), this will also open up, what is referred to by the *Mardukite Academy* as, the *"Infinity Grade."* [For instructional purposes, we tend to still refer to a practitioner as a *"Seeker"* in the *upper-level* manuals.]

There is no finite end-point to the *"Infinity Grade"* because its ultimate goal is the *"increase of spiritual perception,"* which is, in essence, *unlimited.* This means that plenty of room remains for future researchers to contribute; but only after first completing their *Advanced Training* regarding the parts of our *"Map"* that are *already* researched, well-plotted, effective in application, and thus published.

A *Seeker* could complete *A.T. Manual #3,* and then move on directly to *Level-8* with *A.T. Manual #5* (*"Entities & Fragments"*). If, however, a *Seeker* doesn't have enough *"reality"* on that *Level-8* material—as in, it doesn't seem *"real"* enough to them—then some time studying *A.T. Manual #4* (*"Implanted Universes"*) may be of benefit. The covert purpose of introducing *"Implant Platforms #1-18" (AT#3)* and the *"IPU Platforms" (AT#4)* at *Level-7,* is really to make *"Entities & Fragments" (AT#5)* more accessible.

To apply *upper-level Systemology,* an *advanced Seeker* must follow the prescribed outline of instruction that is now available for the first time to the public as the *"Keys to the Kingdom"* series.

Advanced Manuals should be studied in the sequential order in which they are numbered.

Keep these prerequisite materials accessible:
PC Lesson-1 to 16; Processing-Levels 0 to 6
AT Manual #1, "The Secret of Universes"
AT Manual #2, "Games, Goals & Purposes"
AT Manual #3, "The Jewel of Knowledge"
AT Manual #4, "Implanted Universes"
AT Manual #5, "Entities & Fragments"
AT Manual #6, "Spiritual Perception"

Review this prerequisite material:
PC Lesson-13, "Spiritual Energy"
PC Lesson-16, "Alpha Thought"

A.T. MANUAL #7
MASTERING
ASCENSION

SELF-DIRECTION & INTENTION

There are many *"New Age"* publications and *"pop-spirituality"* seminars that emphasize various *"secrets of attraction"* and *"powers of intention," &tc.* This is primarily because all modern *"New Age"* and *"new consciousness"* material is an extension of the *"New Thought"* movement developing in America during the late 1800s and early 1900s—combined with the influence of a *"magical (magickal) revival"* simultaneously occurring in Europe, where *"Will"* became the new *sacred name* for *Self.*

Increasing *"personal horsepower"* behind *"focused intention" is* a critical component for progressive development on the *Pathway* to *Self-Actualizing* as an *"Ascended Master."* It is not, however, the direct emphasis of earlier *processing-levels,* which focus on more general *defragmentation* of the *Mind-System* and the *Human Condition.* We have specific *systematic* reasons for handling the *Pathway* in this way.

Much like *"Alpha-Thought"* (see *PC-16*), a true and original *"cause-point"* or *"source-point"* of *Intention* is always *"exterior-to," "senior"* to, or otherwise *"beyond"* the level of *Beta-Existence* and even the *Mind-System.* It is plotted at "5" on the *Standard Model* (*ZU-Line*).

At an *Alpha-level, Intention* is a resulting product, expression, or manifestation of *Alpha-Thought*; similar to how *Effort* is a resulting product of *Thought* in *Beta-Existence.* Typically, the *standard-issue Human* is not operating by *direct Intention* in *Beta-Existence,* but instead, *via* (or *through*) a *fragmented Mind-System.*

A *"communication"* or *"postulate"* is directed by the *Alpha-Spirit* along the *ZU-Line.* The first "communicable expression" of this—outside one's own *Personal Universe*

—is an *Intention.* The *Alpha-Spirit* has already *postulated* that "something" exists (or "*Is*") and can now *intend* "something" about it. This is how things directly operated in earlier *Universes,* before the *condensation* and *solidity* of both a *Mind* and *Existence.*

While operating in *this Universe,* on *Earth,* and with the *Human Condition,* we are not in the habit of *knowingly Self-Directing Intention* toward *bodies* and other *energetic-mass.* In most cases, these *Intentions* are simply "absorbed" by the convoluted *circuitry* and *machinery* of a *Mind-System* (as a *receipt-point* and *relay*).

Once the *communication* of our original *Intention* has "sputtered" around the *considerations* and *reality-agreements* of the *Mind* for a while, it eventually results in (*Self* + *Body*) experiencing some state of "*Beta-Awareness*" before manifesting as an *effort* (with a *Body*) toward the *action* of using "*force*" in *Beta-Existence.*

A pure *Intention* originates from a *consideration-of-beingness*—or even a *viewpoint*—that is *"exterior-to"* the *Mind-Body* considerations. Anything else and we are not really handling *Intention*; we would be handling *reactive-imagery* and *associative thought* of the programmed, conditioned, and implanted *Mind-System*.

When effectively applied, previous *processing* will have mostly *cleared the way* for *Intention* to be directly *communicated*. This is when a *Seeker/Wizard* can start putting greater emphasis on increasing the *"power"* or *"volume"* of those *Intentions*. Alternating working on this and other *upper-level processing* (*"Implants"* and *"Entities"*).

This *Advanced Training* manual (*AT#7*) presents material *Wizard Level-3X*. As of early 2024, this *level* is still in its "experimental stage" (hence the "X")—but it is sufficiently developed for standard release in the *"Keys to the Kingdom" A.T.*

series. [As other "higher" (still theoretical) gradients of the *Wizard-Levels* are researched, some material found here may be added to, altered, or altogether reassigned to another *level*.]

INTENTION: DIRECTING THOUGHT (*Wizard Level-3X Keynote Lecture*)

Having treated *"Entities"* in *A.T. Manual #5*, and *"Ejection"* (*Wizard Level-1*) and *"Perception"* (*Wizard Level-2*) in *A.T. Manual #6*, we arrive at *Wizard Level-3X*: *"Intention."*

To most effectively progress with *Wizard Level-3X*: a *Seeker* should *alternate* between practicing *"objective"* exercises of *"Intention-On-Mass"* and *processing-sessions* spent *defragmenting* the *considerations* (and other *inhibitors* and *suppressors*) *of "Intention."* The frequency of *alternating*—how often or when—is at a *Seeker's* own discretion to determine for their case.

The basic experimental *"processing routine"* given for *Wizard Level-3X* (in this manual) is fairly *self-guiding* and easily applied by a *Level-8 systemologist.* Therefore, the part we will lead off with for our opening instruction pertains to the potential *systematic* application of other *"objective"* exercises to *standard procedure.*

<u>"INTENTION-ON-MASS"</u> (*WIZ-3X*)

This *"objective exercise"* formula is meant as only *one* part of the complete *Wizard Level-3X* routine. The *other* part is directly *processing-out fragmented considerations* and *postulates*—and other inhibiting factors, such as *Implants* and *Entities.* This cannot be overstated, because a *Seeker* is likely to take a greater interest in, and put more significance on, the *"objective exercises"* right from the start.

The real purpose of *Wizard Level-3X* is to increase certainty on the *ability* to focus and *communicate* a clear *Intention*—which is to say:

1. certainty that a focused *communication*
2. has *arrived* at its *intended "receipt-point"* (or *"effect-point"*)
3. and is *"duplicated"* there, perfectly (accurately) with the "meaning" originally *intended*; for which
4. it is *acknowledged* as having happened.

That is the basic *"communication-cycle"* a *Seeker* should follow when applying *objective exercises*. And it *is* a full *"cycle"* that a *Seeker* should observe. The individual *projects* an *Intention* on a *communication-line* as the *"source-point"* (or *Cause*). They must also be *willing-to-be* the *"receipt-point"* to *perceive* a *"response."*

Our emphasis is on certainty (without question) that a *communicated Intention* is *received*. While this can be *"coached,"* it is not easily *Co-Piloted.* A *Seeker* is typically their own best "judge" on the degree of certainty they have regarding *Intention* and remaining follow-through of the *cycle.*

A *Seeker's* approach to *Wizard Level-3X* must remain *systematic.* We are treating *upper-level* subjects that are too easily *invalidated* by other individuals and the *Physical Universe.* We must keep the aforementioned goals for this *level* in view, rather than invalidating our *gains* and abandoning the *Pathway* simply because *objects* in the room don't just start *"floating all around"* on *command.*

The *Systemology Society "research division"* reviewed a tremendous amount of *"New Age," "New Thought"* and *"para-psychological"* material pertaining to *"telekinesis"* for the development of *Wizard Level-3X*—little of which was *systematically applicable* to our purposes, but it provided a place to start.

First of all, the *"para-scientific"* fields exploring this previously have misappropriated the *"source-point"* of *Intention* as the *Mind* (such as *"mind over matter"*), when all *spiritual abilities* are those originating with the *Alpha-Spirit* and *Alpha Thought*—not a *Mind*.

Technically speaking: standard *circuitry* (*Implanting, &tc.*) of the *Mind-System* is a *barrier* that an *Alpha-Spirit* must properly *dissolve* or *disperse* in order to get their *Intention* clearly across. *Intention* is an *Alpha*-quality that is roughly equivalent to *"effort"* in *Beta-Existence,* which is why *direct-intention* can mimic the *effects* of *effort* in *this Physical Universe*.

Secondly, by *"telekinetic ability,"* we mean affecting the *energetic-mass* of *Beta-Existence* "remotely" by *Intention* (without direct intervention/*effort* applied by a *body,* or some other "physical" means). Indeed, *"levitation"* is one key example of this. And while it *is* contrary to, or in *disagree-*

ment with, *reality-agreements* maintaining *this Physical Universe,* such was not the case for *Alpha-Spirits* in previous *Universes* (versions of *Beta-Existence*).

Thirdly, we considered *mirroring* the "experimental procedures" from various research organizations that study the *telekinetic* phenomenon of "moving things with one's mind." These procedures are similar to what you see in movies with "paranormal investigators." In most cases, an *"ashtray"* is set on a table. It has a "circle" drawn around it and the individual focuses on moving the *ashtray* out of the "circle."

We liked the idea of the *ashtray;* we disliked the activity itself as a *systematic process* or exercise. For one, it limited the idea of practicing with *alternating Intentions,* when about all you could really say to the thing is *"move"* or *"move"* repeatedly. The other concern was the *invalidation issue*—setting up a hidden standard for personal gains where the only achievement of success possible is spontaneous "action-at-a-distance."

The *ashtray,* however, *is* an appropriate *object* for instructing this type of *objective* exercise.

1. It is a *receptacle* by design. For *"consideration"* and *"visualization"* sake, this allows a *Seeker* to more easily conceive of directing *Intention* not only *into* the "substance" of the *object,* but also *"filling"* it, and *permeating* its *Space.*

2. It is of *moderate size* to focus attention on; preferably colored-*glass,* rather than *plastic* or *transparent.*

3. It is *lightweight,* which makes it easy to physically handle during exercises.

Practice of this exercise will not be unusual to an experienced *Seeker.* We previously demonstrated other variations of this technique—for example, when the PCL called for "making objects feel an emotion," *&tc*. However, in previous *processing-levels,* we did not particularly address the *Intention,* or emphasize the *"communication-cycle"* that ensues for the exercise to be truly effective as a *systematic process*.

The following *formula* identifies the *"communication-cycle."* A *Seeker* should work toward developing the highest possible *certainty* on these basic points during their practice:

0. *Forming a clear "Intention"—thinking* a *'Thought'*;
1. *Directing the Intention toward, inside, and all around, the object;*
2. *Knowing that the Intention (command, communication, &tc.) has been received;*
3. *Perceiving the response, feedback, or effect-action taking place.*
4. *Acknowledging that the response (&tc.) has been received.*

There are two *"intended commands"* directed toward the *object* in this *systematic* version of other methods. They are: *"Rise Up!"* and *"Set Down!"* The *acknowledgment* that is given to end either *cycle* is *"Thank You!"*

To validate that there is *feedback* or *effect* for this exercise: after there is certainty that the directed *Intention* to *"Rise Up"* is received, the *Seeker* physically *lifts* the *object* up; and after *"Set Down,"* they *set* it back down.

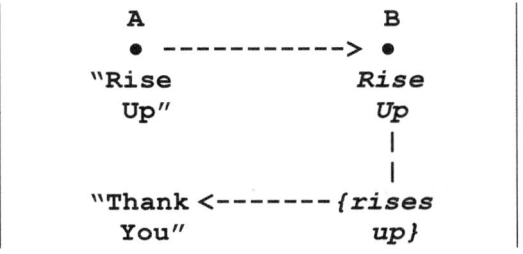

```
    A                    B
    • ------------> •
 "Rise                 Rise
   Up"                  Up
                         |
                         |
 "Thank <--------{rises
   You"                 up}
```

The basic instruction for this exercise is no more complicated than this. To provide variation to the practice, we suggest:

1. commands *intended* out loud;
2. commands *intended* silently; and
3. *Intentions* given with nonsense words.

ADDITIONAL DATA ON LEVITATION

An occurrence of the actual at-a-distance phenomenon of *"telekinesis"* or *"levitation"* is *not* one of the prescribed *Wizard Level-3X* end-goals. This does not exclude the possibility for a *Wizard-Level Seeker* to achieve it; but it is not how we measure personal success for this gradient of *upper-level* work.

Based on our experimental and research data: if and when a *Seeker* experiences this phenomenon, it will occur without any actual *effort* or *strain*—or any other *forced intensity* behind the directed *Intention*—and to accomplish "on command," would require being in perfect *communication* with the *target-object*.

Although we have not yet treated the

subject of *"energy"* directly for the *Wizard-Levels,* it can already be determined that the matter of *"levitation"* (*&tc.*) is not a concern of *"having enough energy"* to physically move the *mass.*

The *Alpha-Spirit* has unlimited ability to *create "Energy"* at will, which is only hindered by other *considerations* about *"energy-sources"* and *"restrictive uses"* (*&tc.*) that are specific to *this Universe.* In spite of this, for our *practice exercises,* it is still better to work with *mass* that can be easily handled (like an *ashtray*). Working with heavier *masses* may just *"pull-in"* additional *considerations* regarding one's physical abilities.

This all being said: the primary focus of *Wizard Level-3X Procedure* is *processing willingness, reach,* and *responsibility,* to increase clarity of *Intention* and the certainty of *being-at-Cause.*

WIZARD LEVEL-3X PROCEDURE (*Example–Intention: Levitation*)

Start each *session* by *running "Preventative Fundamentals"* (*PC-9*). Now that we are treating specific subjects or areas at *Level-8*, it might be helpful to also check *"Preventative Fundamentals"* on any accessible *entities* that may get *"restimulated"* or *"intrusively active"* regarding *"Levitation."* This is done by addressing the surrounding area, usually with a *Biofeedback-Device* (after any personal *"Meter-reads"* on the word *"Levitation"* are *defragmented*).

This *upper-level* procedure utilizes virtually all *Systemology processing* theories in a single routine. It is applied to the example for which we have been discussing —*"Intention: Levitation"*—but its formula could be easily modified to *process-out* innumerable other areas as well.

A. <u>ANALYTICAL RECALL</u>

Run the PCL as *Basic (Light) Recall.* Cycle through each set-of-three a few times before going to the next. Since access to the *Backtrack* may be currently limited, if you are unable to directly *"recall"* what is asked for, *consider* the first *"idea"* or *"mental image"* that occurs. If nothing is *resurfacing* or "coming to mind," simply *"Imagine"* a scenario for that *item-line.*

PCL = *"Recall a time..."*

1a. *"you enjoyed levitating something."*
1b. *"another enjoyed you levitating something."*
1c. *"another enjoyed others levitating something."*

2a. *"you disliked levitating something."*
2b. *"you disliked another levitating something."*
2c. *"another disliked others levitating something."*

3a. *"you levitated something because you thought it was important."*

3b. *"you felt it was important for another to levitate."*

3c. *"another felt it was important for others to levitate."*

4a. *"you levitated something to create a good effect."*

4b. *"you felt it created a good effect for another to levitate."*

4c. *"another felt it created a good effect for others to levitate."*

5a. *"you could levitate something, but chose not to."*

5b. *"another could levitate something, but chose not to."*

5c. *"others could levitate something, but chose not to."*

6a. *"you levitated something and it improved communication."*

6b. *"another levitated something and it improved communication."*

6c. *"others levitated something and it improved communication."*

7a. *"you levitated something and it made people like you better."*

7b. *"another levitated something and it made people like them better."*

7c. *"others levitated something and it made people like them better."*

B. <u>BASIC CONSIDERATIONS/DECISIONS</u>

Run the PCL:

1. *"Recall some decisions you have made about levitating."*
2. *"Recall some decisions someone else has made about levitating."*
3. *"Recall some decisions others have made about levitating."*
4. *"Write down some bad effects you could create by levitating."*
5. *"Write down some good effects you could create by levitating."*
6. *"Write down some games you would spoil by levitating."*
7. *"Write down some new games you could have by levitating."*

C. HELP

One of the reasons an *Alpha-Spirit* restrains their abilities is because they don't believe that it will *help* others, or it is connected to times when they have *failed-to-help*. We focus on the more positive aspects in this *basic process,* rather than *resurfacing* "trauma." But we still must treat the *considerations* from both sides: *"levitating"* and *"not-levitating."*

1. *"How could you help another by not-levitating?"*
2. *"How could another help you by not-levitating?"*
3. *"How could another help others by not-levitating?"*
4. *"How could another help themselves by not-levitating?"*
5. *"How could you help yourself by not-levitating?"*
6. *"How could you help another by levitating?"*
7. *"How could another help you by levitating?"*

8. *"How could another help others by levitating?"*
9. *"How could another help themselves by levitating?"*
10. *"How could you help yourself by levitating?"*

D. PROBLEMS AND SOLUTIONS

Run the PCL (repeat as needed):

1a. *"Spot a problem that not-levitating would solve."*
1b. *"How would that be a solution?"*
2a. *"Spot a problem that another/others might solve by not-levitating."*
2b. *"How would that be a solution?"*
3a. *"Spot a problem that you might solve by preventing others from levitating."*
3b. *"How would that be a solution?"*
4a. *"Spot a problem that you might solve for others by not-levitating."*
4b. *"How would that be a solution?"*

E. <u>PROBLEMS AND RESISTANCE</u>

This *process* illustrates another angle for addressing *considerations-of-problems.* It follows the theory that an individual must *be resisting against* "the other side" (and therefore feeding it *attention* and *energy*) in order to be *fixated* on a *"problem."* *Run* the PCL (repeat "b" a number of times to answer "a"):

1a. *"Spot a problem that you could have with levitation."*

1b. *"What would you have to 'resist' (or 'be resisting') to consider that a problem?"*

2a. *"Spot a problem that someone else could have with levitation."*

2b. *"What would they have to 'resist' (or 'be resisting') to consider that a problem?"*

3a. *"Spot a problem that others could have with levitation."*

3b. *"What would they have to 'resist' (or 'be resisting') to consider that a problem?"*

F. CONNECTEDNESS/SEPARATENESS

Alternate the PCL within each set:

1a. *"Spot an object in the room."*
1b. *"Get a sense of being connected with it."*
1c. *"Get a sense of being separate from it."*
{alternate (1b) and (1c)}

2a. *"Spot objects in the room that you would be willing to connect with."*
2b. *"Spot objects in the room that you would be willing to make connect with you."*

3a. *"Spot objects in the room that you are separate from."*
3b. *"Spot objects in the room that are separate from you."*

G. INVALIDATION

This *process* is *run* like checking *"Preventative Fundamentals"* on a *GSR-Meter* for any *"charge"* that *registers.* For each *Meter-reading-item,* you *"Spot {'What Is'}"* for that item until it *discharges/disperses* on *realization.*

1. *"On 'Levitation'; have you invalidated yourself?"*
2. *"On 'Levitation'; has another/others invalidated themselves?"*
3. *"On 'Levitation'; have you been invalidated by another?"*
4. *"On 'Levitation'; have you invalidated another/others?"*
5. *"On 'Levitation'; has another invalidated others?"*
6. *"On 'Levitation'; have you gotten another/others to invalidate themselves?"*

H. RESISTANCE/WILLINGNESS

This practices directing (putting or placing) a *"thought"* or *"concept"* (*Intention*) into an *object*. Repeat with many *objects*.

1. *"Spot an object in the room."*

2a. *"Put into it 'a resistance to being levitated'."*

2b. *"Put into it 'a willingness to being levitated'."*

{alternate (2a) and (2b) on *object*}

I. CAUSE/BLAME

This is partly an *"imaginative process."* It requires perceiving (receiving) a *"response"* or *"intention"* (*communication*) from an *object*. [Of course, the whole thing occurs based on your own Intention to *create* (or *Imagine*) and getting the sense of it occurring.] Alternate (2a) and (2b); but *run* one several times before shifting to the other. Repeat with many *objects*.

1. *"Spot an object in the room."*
2a. *"Have it looking up at you with admiration for being Cause."*
2b. *"Have it looking up to blame you."*

J. HARMFUL-ACTS/HOLD-BACKS

Harmful-Acts lead to *Hold-Backs* (see *PC-6*), which are a major contributor to compulsively restraining abilities. Since access to the *Backtrack* may be currently limited, if you are unable to directly *"Spot"* what is asked for, *consider* the first *"idea"* or *"mental image"* that occurs. If nothing is *resurfacing* or "coming to mind," simply *"Imagine"* a scenario for that *item-line. Spot* many examples for each:

1. *"Spot an act of harming something by levitating."*
2. *"Spot a harmful-act of preventing others from levitating."*
3. *"Spot times when you regretted having levitated something. If necessary, scan the incident in reverse; Spot the harmful-act 'As-It-Is' and defragment-by-realization."*
4. *"Spot times you had justification for stopping others from levitating. Write down any of these 'justification considerations'. Check for an earlier harmful-act against the terminal (others) or against you (if you do think you were really justified in stopping them)."*

K. <u>VALIDATION-FOR-INABILITY</u>

Often times, if an individual is *not* using

an *ability,* it is because they *consider* themselves as getting *more validation* (from others) for *not* using the *ability. Run* the PCL for *considerations*:

1. *"How could you validate someone else for not-levitating?"*
2. *"How could someone else validate you for not-levitating?"*
3. *"How could others validate others for not-levitating?"*

L. <u>HARMFUL-ACTS AND SOLUTIONS</u>

In previous *Universes, levitation-abilities* allowed for so much "trouble" that we worked very hard at preventing it with the *reality-agreements* of *this Physical Universe.* Much of our own *agreement* to these conditions involves trying to solve the problem of others being able to *levitate* as a means to *harmful-acts.*

1a. *"Write down a harmful-act you could commit against another/others by levitating."*

1b. *"How would that be solved or prevented?"*

2a. *"Write down a harmful-act another/ others could commit against you by levitating."*

2b. *"How would that be solved or prevented?"*

3a. *"Write down a harmful-act another could commit against others by levitating."*

3b. *"How would that be solved or prevented?"*

4a. *"Write down a harmful-act you could commit against yourself by levitating."*

4b. *"How would that be solved or prevented?"*

M. <u>MENTAL REACH</u>

This is an *"objective exercising"* break from the previous, more *subjective, processes.* Simply *"Spot objects in the room"* and *"mentally reach and let-go (from each one) three times."*

N. <u>ALPHA-THOUGHT/POSTULATES</u>

Alternate the PCL:

1. *"Spot/Recall some postulates you have made about levitation."*
2. *"Spot/Recall some postulates someone else has made about levitating."*
3. *"Spot/Recall some postulates others have made about levitating."*
4. *"Spot/Recall some postulates you have made about another/others levitating."*

O. <u>JUSTIFICATION CONSIDERATIONS</u>

This is a *listing* exercise. If you are using a *Biofeedback-Device,* then you can check your *listed-items* for *Meter-reads.* Even if there is no significant *fragmented-charge* on all of these PCL-prompted *considerations*: simply use it for *light processing; listing* basic *considerations.* [Note: all of these PCL are looking to target the *same "justification"* from different angles.]

1a. *"How could you make yourself right by not-levitating?"*

1b. *"How could you make others wrong by not-levitating?"*

2a. *"How could you make yourself right by preventing levitation?"*

2b. *"How could you make others wrong by preventing levitation?"*

If you have difficulty with listing on these, consider the following approach:

"How could 'not-levitating' (or 'preventing-levitation') earn you 'sympathy' from others?"

P. <u>WILLINGNESS</u>

One reason we *hold-back* our *ability* to *levitate* is because we don't want others to do it. On the *Backtrack,* things could easily get "out-of-control" when this *ability* was standard.

With the way our *reality-agreements* and *considerations* for *existence* are structured: we are not going to be *fully willing* to *levitate* unless we are *fully willing* to grant others the right to use that *ability* as well.

The basic PCL for this *process* ("b") must each be alternated with *"willingness-for-Self"* ("a") in order to keep the *process running*.

1a. *"Look around and spot an object you would be willing to move."*
1b. *"Look around and spot an object you would be willing for someone else to move."*
2a. *"Look around and spot an object you would be willing to move."*
2b. *"Look around and spot an object you would be willing for an Alpha-Spirit to move."*
3a. *"Look around and spot an object you would be willing to move."*
3b. *"Look around and spot an object you would be willing for a Bonded-Entity to move."*
4a. *"Look around and spot an object you would be willing to move."*
4b. *"Look around and spot an object you would be willing to have move by itself."*

Q. NEGATIVE-LOCATIONAL

This *process* is *run* to loosen-up *compulsive machinery.*

1. *"Spot some places where you are not."*
2. *"Spot some places where you don't have to levitate."*
3. *"Spot some places where another doesn't have to levitate."*
4. *"Spot some objects you don't have to levitate."*
5. *"Spot some objects another doesn't have to levitate."*
6. *"Spot some people you don't have to stop from levitating things."*
7. *"Spot some people that someone else doesn't have to stop from levitating things."*
8. *"Spot some objects you don't have to hold still."*
9. *"Spot some objects someone else doesn't have to hold still."*

R. "MUST-NOT-TOUCH"

Alternate each PCL-set several times.

1a. *"Spot an object in the room."*

1b. *"As your attention fixes on it, have it say: 'Must Not Touch'."*

2a. *"Spot an object in the room."*

2b. *"As your attention fixes on it, you say to it: 'Must Not Touch'."*

3a. *"Spot an object in the room."*

3b. *"Put an energy-beam on it with your attention, and have the walls say: 'Must Not Touch'."*

4a. *"Spot an object in the room."*

4b. *"Put an energy-beam on it with your attention, and you tell the walls: 'Must Not Touch'."*

S. ACTS/HOLD-BACKS (6TH SPHERE)

Alternate each PCL-set several times.

1a. *"What have you done to an environment?"*

1b. *"What have you held-back from an environment?"*

2a. *"What has someone else done to an environment?"*

2b. *"What has someone else held-back from an environment?"*

3a. *"What have others done to an environment?"*

3b. *"What have others held-back from an environment?"*

T. <u>ACTS/JUSTIFICATION (6TH SPHERE)</u>

Alternate each PCL-set several times.

1a. *"What have you done to objects?"*

1b. *"How have you justified that?"*

2a. *"What have you done to energies?"*

2b. *"How have you justified that?"*

3a. *"What have you done to spaces?"*

3b. *"How have you justified that?"*

4a. *"What have you done to the future of an environment?"*

4b. *"How have you justified that?"*

U. <u>CAUSE/HOLD-BACKS (6TH SPHERE)</u>

Alternate each PCL-set several times.

1a. *"What could you cause to happen to an object?"*

1b. *"What could you hold-back from doing to an object?"*

2a. *"What could someone else cause to happen to an object?"*

2b. *"What could someone else hold-back from doing to an object?"*

3a. *"What could you cause to happen to an energy?"*

3b. *"What could you hold-back from doing to an energy?"*

4a. *"What could someone else cause to happen to an energy?"*

4b. *"What could someone else hold-back from doing to an energy?"*

5a. *"What could you cause to happen to a space?"*

5b. *"What could you hold-back from doing to a space?"*

6a. *"What could someone else cause to happen to a space?"*
6b. *"What could someone else hold-back from doing to a space?"*
7a. *"What could you postulate into an object's future?"*
7b. *"What could you hold-out from postulating into an object's future?"*
8a. *"What could someone else postulate into an object's future?"*
8b. *"What could someone else hold-out from postulating into an object's future?"*

V. <u>CONSEQUENCES</u>

We have discussed *"reality-agreements"* and *"Monitor-Entities"* in previous *A.T. Manuals*. An individual is likely to have a "sense of" the idea that performing something like *levitation* would "break the rules" and one would be in "trouble" with some kind of "super-force," *&tc.* Therefore, a *Seeker* may be holding onto some *highly charged considerations* concerning anticipated consequences to *levitation.*

The first PCL is for *listing*. After writing down answers, see if any *register* on a *GSR-Meter* (or feel as though they have *fragmented charge* attached to them). Continue the *process* with the remaining PCL until you get a sense of *relief*—or greater certainty of *being-at-Cause*—regarding the situation; then return to ("1").

1. *"What horrible thing might happen if you levitated an object?"*
2. *"Create a mental image picture of the horrible thing happening out in front of you."*
3. *"Make it more solid."*
4. *"Copy it many times; make each copy more solid."*
5. *"Make more copies; change the colors and move things around in the scenery."*
6. *"Push some copies into the Body; throw some copies away into the distance."*

W. <u>HIGH-PRESSURE TRAPS</u>

On the *Backtrack,* sometimes *objects* were set up to "explode" or "implode" when you touched them—either as a stand-alone *"trap,"* or to reduce one's *Actualized Awareness* during an *Implant*. Alternate each PCL-set several times.

1a. *"Spot an object in the room."*
1b. *"Put an energy-beam on it with your attention; and imagine the object exploding."*
2a. *"Spot an object in the room."*
2b. *"Imagine someone else putting an energy-beam on it; and the object exploding."*
3a. *"Spot an object in the room."*
3b. *"Put an energy-beam on it with your attention; and imagine it imploding (pulling at you with a vacuum suction)."*
4a. *"Spot an object in the room."*
4b. *"Imagine someone else putting an energy-beam on it; and the object imploding (pulling them into the*

vacuum suction)."

X. <u>POSITIVE-LOCATIONAL</u>

1. *"From where could you levitate an object?"*
2. *"From where could someone else levitate an object?"*

Y. <u>THOUGHT-BARRIERS</u>

Check the following areas for *fragmented charge.* For each *Meter-reading-item* (or if you sense *turbulence* for an area): *"Spot {'What Is'}"* for that *item* until it *discharges/disperses* on *realization.*

1. *"Getting someone to stop levitating your things by convincing them that only you can levitate the things that you have created."*
2. *"Deciding that: since you can't levitate things, you are going to make certain that no one else can either."*
3. *"Being ordered to levitate something that you don't want to, and avoiding it by demonstrating that you can't really do it."*

4. *"Deciding (or being convinced) that: you shouldn't levitate objects because it sets a bad example for other people with poor control, who would try to do it in foolish ways and mess things up."*

Z. ENERGY (BASIC RECALL)

Before *running* the PCL: check *Preventative Fundamentals* specifically *"On Using Energy"* (both for *Self* and accessible *entities*).

1. *"Recall controlling energy."*
2. *"Recall someone else controlling energy."*
3. *"Recall others controlling energy."*

AA. CONTROLLING ENERGY

This is an *objective exercise*. It is practiced while walking around your home, *&tc*. Practice with "water faucets" that have a visible *flow* (*the water*) before handling "light-switches" or "electrical flows."

1. *"Start and stop energy-flows by turning things 'on' and 'off'."*

2. *"Take notice of the flow when you turn something 'on'; and the no-flow when you turn something 'off'."*

BB. HARMFUL-ACTS/HOLD-BACKS

Run the *processes* for STEP-J; but replace *"levitating"* (or *"levitating something"*) with *"Creating Energy"* (for the PCL).

CC. VALIDATION-FOR-INABILITY

Run the *processes* for STEP-K; but replace *"not-levitating"* with *"not-Creating Energy"* (for the PCL).

DD. HARMFUL-ACTS AND SOLUTIONS

Run the *processes* for STEP-L; but replace *"levitating"* with *"Creating Energy"* (for the PCL).

EE. ENERGY (GENERAL)

1. *"Spot some places where you are not."*
2. *"Spot some places where energy is not."*
3. *"Spot some energy that is not currently hitting you."*

4. *"Spot some places where you are not putting energy."*
5. *"Spot some energy that you could have."*
6. *"Spot some energy that you could permit to remain where it is."*
7. *"Spot some energy that you could permit to disperse."*
8. *"Spot some energy that you could disagree with."*
9. *"Spot some energy that you could agree with if it suddenly appeared."*

FF. <u>OWNERSHIP-OF-ENERGY</u>

1. *"Spot some energies that you could own."*
2. *"Spot some energies that you would be willing for another to own."*
3. *"Spot some energies that you would be willing to give to another."*
4. *"Spot some energies that you would be willing for another to give to you."*
5. *"Spot some energies that you would be willing for another to give to others."*

GG. PUTTING-ENERGY-IN-WALLS

Practices of "putting" (*projecting/directing*) *"thoughts"* and *"concepts"* into *Walls* is a standard method of *processing-out compulsive "machinery."* However, just putting the *"idea"* of *heat, cold, electricity,* or *radiation,* into *Walls* is not as *systematically* effective as with other applications of this technique.

In *this Physical Universe,* such energetic manifestations are the result of *"particle motion."* Therefore, when this type of exercise is applied to the concept of *Energy* (*heat, &tc.*), it is important to also add the *creation/imagining* of the *"particles-in-motion"* to that *Energy-type.*

HH. FALLING-UPWARDS (GRAVITY)

The basic PCL for this exercise are:

1. *"Get a sense of falling upwards."*
2. *"Get a sense of other things falling upwards."*

A *Seeker* should stay on one PCL to get a real certainty on their *"sense"* or *"impression"* before shifting.

Variations of this exercise include:

1. *Create/Imagine various objects on the ground outdoors, one at a time, at an increasing scale of size (ashtrays, books, boxes, furniture, automobiles, aircrafts, &tc.); then have them "fall upwards" into the sky and outer space.*
2. *Spot objects in the room. For each one in turn: create/imagine a copy of it "falling upwards" through the ceiling, into the sky.*
3. *Eject-Awareness and spot large objects, one at a time, around the planet (buildings, monuments, mountains, &tc.); then Imagine them "falling upwards" into the sky and outer space.*

II. <u>"CAN'T-DO-THAT"</u>

Alternate each PCL-set several times.

1a. *"Spot an object in the room."*
1b. *"Put an energy-beam on it with your*

attention, and have it say: 'You Can't Do That'."

2a. *"Spot an object in the room."*
2b. *"Put an energy-beam on it with your attention, and you say to it: 'You Can't Do That'."*

3a. *"Spot an object in the room."*
3b. *"Put an energy-beam on it with your attention, and have the walls, floor, and ceiling, laugh while saying: 'You Can't Do That'."*

4a. *"Spot an object in the room."*
4b. *"Put an energy-beam on it with your attention, and you laugh while telling the walls, floor, and ceiling: 'You Can't Do That'."*

JJ. <u>SPOILING-THE-GAME (TRUST)</u>

Alternate a PCL-set, then shift.

1a. *"Spot an object in the room."*
1b. *"Decide to levitate it because you can; then decide not to because it would spoil-the-game."*

2a. *"Spot some people you could trust with the ability to levitate."*
2b. *"Spot some people who would be safe if you had the ability to levitate."*

KK. <u>INTERIORIZING-EJECTION</u>

Alternate a PCL-set, then shift.

1a. *"Spot an object in the room."*
1b. *"Interiorize into it; then eject out from it."* {*repeat several times*}
2a. *"Spot an object in the room."*
2b. *"Imagine/visualize other Alpha-Spirits interiorizing into it and ejecting out of it."*

LL. <u>CONCEPTUAL-CERTAINTY</u>

Uncertainty—the *"lack of certainty"*—reduces an individual's *Actualized Awareness* by suspending their *attention* on a perpetual "maybe." This is accomplished (often with *Implanting*) by holding an intense *energetic-charge* on two *opposing considerations* about a specific *concept*. For example, if equally *charged*: *"I can do.."* and *"I can't do.."* would keep an individual in a state of partial *unknowingness* about their abilities.

Alternate the two PCL of a set before going to the next. Make sure that you *really "get a sense"* of what each PCL calls for (rather than a vague idea).

1a. *"Get a certainty that objects can be levitated."*
1b. *"Get a certainty that objects cannot be levitated."*
2a. *"Get a certainty that you can levitate objects."*
2b. *"Get a certainty that you cannot levitate objects."*
3a. *"Get a certainty that others can levitate objects."*
3b. *"Get a certainty that others cannot levitate objects."*
4a. *"Get a certainty that you can generate energetic-force."*

4b. *"Get a certainty that you cannot generate energetic-force."*
5a. *"Get a certainty that others can generate energetic-force."*
5b. *"Get a certainty that others cannot generate energetic-force."*
6a. *"Get a certainty that you must levitate things."*
6b. *"Get a certainty that you must not levitate things."*

MM. INTENTION-ON-PEOPLE

Run this *process* in a public place (where people are visible). If this is not convenient when reaching this step of the procedure: continue to the next step and return to this *process* when it can be completed.

The purpose of this *process* is to loosen one's fixed *postulates* and *reality-agreements*. It is *run* by *postulating* (or *imagining/visualizing*) opposing *"ideas"* (or *Intentions*) and "putting" (*placing/project-*

ing) them into others. [This is *run* silently by *Intention*.]

1a. *"Postulate 'an inability to levitate' into people."*

1b. *"Postulate 'an ability to levitate' into people."*

2a. *"Grant people 'the right to levitate'."*

2b. *"Imagine people granting you 'the right to levitate'."*

3a. *"Postulate 'a lack of energy' into people."*

3b. *"Postulate 'an abundance of energy' into people."*

3c. *"Postulate 'being a source of energy' into people."*

4a. *"Grant people 'the right to generate energy'."*

4b. *"Imagine people granting you 'the right to generate energy'."*

5a. *"Postulate 'a lack of havingness' into people."*

5b. *"Postulate 'an abundance of havingness' into people."*

5c. *"Postulate 'being a source of havingness' into people."*

6a. *"Grant people 'the right to create mass'."*

6b. *"Imagine people granting you 'the right to create mass'."*

7a. *"Postulate 'a lack of space' (or collapsed space) into people."*

7b. *"Postulate 'an abundance of space' into people."*

7c. *"Postulate 'being a source of space' into people."*

8a. *"Grant people 'the right to generate space'."*

8b. *"Imagine people granting you 'the right to generate space'."*

9a. *"Postulate 'a lack of time' (not enough time) into people."*

9b. *"Postulate 'an abundance of time' into people."*

9c. *"Postulate 'being a source of time' into people."*

10a. *"Grant people 'the right to generate their own independent time'."*

10b. *"Imagine people granting you 'the right to generate your own independent time'."*

NN. <u>MACHINERY AND ENTITIES</u> (*AT#5*)

• Check for any *Programmed Machine Entities* (PME) that are currently:

–*"being levitation machinery"*;
–*"being broken levitation machinery"*; or
–*"being levitation-blocking machinery."*

Use *A.T. Manual #5* to handle each one found (e.g. *Spot being made into a machine; Spot the first time;* run *"Identification Procedure"*). If *Control Entities* (CE) or other types become active (or restimulated) doing this, handle them as well. [This type of *machinery* usually accumulates around the *"Third Eye"* area of the forehead.]

• Check for any PME that are currently:

–*"being machinery that puts out energy-beams"*;

–*"being broken machinery that puts out energy-beams"*; or

–*"being energy-beam-blocking machinery."*

• Check for any *"Watchers" ("Monitors"), "Bonded-Entities,"* or other CE that might be secretly observing you, and reporting on you—particularly if you do any major "rule-breaking activities," such as *levitation.*

Starting at *Level-8,* a *Seeker/Wizard* becomes increasingly aware of whether or not there is anything "focused in" on them from a distance that might be blocking *levitation, generating energy,* and other *spiritual abilities.*

Another way of handling interference is to *"put an energy-beam on the object with your attention"* and then check with a *GSR-Meter* if there are any *entities (&tc.)* opposing, protesting, invalidating, or trying to stop you from *levitating* the *object* in any way. [This is worth checking on for the *ashtray* used in the *"Intention-On-*

Mass" exercise—especially before any attempts to practice it "metaphysically."]

OO. REALITY-POSTULATING

This *process* is based on the theory that an individual (*Alpha-Spirit*) is *continuously* and *compulsively "creating reality"* on an *automatic* basis. Therefore, what a *Seeker* is doing *unknowingly,* we have them practice doing with *intentional-control.*

This is an *objective exercise* that involves *"putting intentions"* (*postulates*) into *objects* found in the room or environment.

PCL = *"Spot an object in the room and..."*

1. *"postulate solidity into it."*
2. *"postulate weight into it."*
3. *"postulate color into it."*
4. *"postulate temperature into it."*
5. *"postulate energy into it."*
6. *"postulate space into it."*
7. *"postulate thought into it."*
8. *"postulate mystery into it."*
9. *"postulate beauty into it."*

10. *"postulate that it has a past (Backtrack) stretching behind it."*
11. *"postulate that it has a future (track) ahead of it."*

PP. <u>TOUCH-AND-GO (COMPONENTS)</u>

This is an extension of the previous *process*. In this step, you select an *object*; then practice *"reaching"* and *"letting-go"* (with your *attention*) of a single specific *"component-quality"* of the *object* (listed in the previous step), such as *weight* or *color, &tc.*

After working through the list several times: repeat the *process*; but this time *"intensify"* or *"increase"* the *component-quality* before *"letting-go."* A basic PCL-formula for this is:

"Reach for the {component-quality}. Increase (or intensify) it; then let go of it."

QQ. <u>"BELL, BOOK & CANDLE"</u> (*PC-3*)

Perform the "physical" and "advanced" versions. [See *PC-3*.]

RR. <u>"CRYSTAL CLEAR"</u> (*Liber-2B*)

Take up a copy of the book *"Crystal Clear: Handbook for Seekers"* and make a pass through the entire text; *run* all *processes* to *total defragmentation* and "end-cycle" on your use (necessity) of that material.

After *running through* this entire procedure (from STEP "A" to "QQ") at least twice—in addition to at least two hours (total among *sessions*) spent practicing *"Intention-On-Mass"*—the *Seeker/Wizard* may then proceed to apply even more *advanced systematic exercises* (from the next section) to their *Wizard Level-3X* routine.

ADVANCED ABILITY TRAINING—3X
(*Example—Intention: Levitation*)

For use after completing standard *"Wizard Level-3X Procedure"* (previous section).

3X-A. "INTENTION-ON-MASS"

[See *"Intention: Directing Thought (Wizard Level-3X Keynote)"* for details.]

3X-B. "BEAMS-ON-A-BODY"

The *Alpha-Spirit* is quite out-of-practice with handling *Energy* and *Force* directly. This exercise practices handling the *Body* using *"energy-beams."* Even above other *mass* in the *Universe,* a *Seeker* would have the greatest certainty of *control* with the *Body* they are currently accustomed to using. [Review the material and exercises from *"Spiritual Energy"* (*PC-13*).]

This exercise is usually practiced after

ejecting-Awareness and standing "outside of, but near to" the *Body*. When operating in this wise, a *Seeker* can get a sense, however slight, of "operating the *Body from* outside the *Body*." Experience with this can improve *"ejection-stability"*—handling *body-motion* while *"exterior to"* the *Body*, without automatically "snapping-in."

This exercise is similar to *"Intention-On-Mass"* (3X-A). We practice "lifting" and "setting down" a bit of *mass*. However, in this case, the *Intention* includes the *creation* and *control* of an *energy-beam* to conduct the action (rather than a strictly verbal-style *"command-intention"* directed at *mass*).

The basic instruction is: "starting with a single finger, practice using *energy-beams* to lift/move the finger, rather than relying on the *Body's* muscles." {more details below}

You can project an *energy-beam* from

"where *you* are" (POV) or from another "remote point." This means an *energy-beam* can be "put out," "projected" or otherwise "postulated" without attaching the other "end" of it to *Self*. For example: a *Seeker* could run *beams* from a spot on the ceiling of a room. A *Seeker* should practice with various approaches to this exercise (as their own personal experiment).

There is a "puppet-master method" of treating *energy-beams* like "wires" or "cables" being handled from "above" (or from the *Alpha-Spirit* while *exterior-to* the *Body*)—and essentially operating the *Body* like a *"marionette-doll."* A more *systematically* accurate approach would involve the *"lengthening"* and *"shortening"* of an *energy-beam "wave"* to control the "tension" or "force"—to either "push" or "pull" on the *beam*.

This exercise begins with a single finger, then works up to a hand, and then an arm. Eventually this can be extended to include all parts of the *Body* simultaneously. When applying *systematic* methods to the *Body,* the best practice is to alternate the side of the *Body* you're working with for each cycle or *session* —"right index finger" then "left index finger," *&tc.*

From previous exercises, a *Seeker* is used to alternating the "putting on" and "pulling off" of *energy-beams.* This is not standard practice when using the *Body* as an *exercise-target* directly. If you repeatedly "put on" and "pull off" *beams* from the *Body,* they have a tendency to get "sticky." Therefore, once *attention* is fixed on the *beam,* the alternation from *"On"* to *"Off"* should be treated like *"Turning It Off"* rather than *"pulling-it-off."*

Similarly to how we manually manipulate motion of an *object* for *"Intention-On-Mass,"* this exercise is *not* expected to set a *Seeker* up for failure or *invalidation*. You can also use "*creativeness processing*" to practice "*imagined*" versions of any gradient or magnitude that exceeds one's reality. For example: if you make good progress with fingers, but not hands, simply spend time *visualizing* the practice you find difficulty with.

Although handling of *energy-beams* is entirely within the scope of *Level-8*, a *Seeker* can treat the exercise as *imaginatively* as necessary, based on their current reality on it, in order to practice it. As with exercise 3X-A, always leave yourself with a "*win*." [In the end, one way or the other: *postulate* that the *finger will lift, &tc.*]

For each part of the *Body* (*finger, &tc.*), practice the following steps:

1. Lay your hand down flat on the table. [For moving the entire arm, lay down and stretch out the entire arm, *&tc.*]
2. *Eject-Awareness*. Float above that part

of the *Body* and fix an *energy-beam* on it with your *attention* (or *by Intention*). Alternate practicing: *"putting the beam on it"/"turning it on"* and *"turning it off."*

3. Put the *beam* on the *body-part* and *"lift it up."* Practice: *"putting the beam on it," "lifting it," "moving the body-part very precisely," "putting it down,"* and *"letting-go"* (*"turning off"* the beam).

3X-C. "4TH-DIMENSIONAL THICKNESS"

Creation and *masses* in *this Physical Universe* are composed of *3-Dimensional structures.* However, there is a slight degree of *"fourth-dimensional thickness"* to its substance. If you were to *imagine* a *2-Dimensional "Flatland"* drawn out on a sheet of paper—the *paper* and *ink,* themselves, would have a slight *3-Dimensional thickness.*

When handling *entities,* you may sometimes perceive a *Bonded-Entity* as a small *"spark"* disappearing in the distance—and yet it doesn't seem to move off very far, relative to our *3-Dimensional Space.* It is essentially moving off into a *fourth-dimensional direction* that is *"sideways"* of the basic *reality* of *this Physical Universe.*

In our practice of *"Reaching for Nothingness"* (and other exercises involving *"direction"*), we tend to work primarily with the *six directions* of our familiar *3-Dimensions*. They are:

left/right; *front/back*; and *up/down*.

Technically, on *Earth,* we treat these as:

east/west; *north/south*; and *up/down*.

They are measured in "geometry" as:

height (or *length*), *width,* and *depth*.

And as the axis-coordinates:

longitude, latitude, and *altitude*.

By a *Fourth-Dimension,* we do not mean what is *postulated* as *"Time"*; we mean a *fourth "spatial" dimension.* This would, by definition, include two additional *"directions."*

Mathematician and writer, *Charles H. Hinton (1853-1907)*, coined the term *"tesseract"* to describe a *"four-dimensional cube."* More specifically to our purposes, he appointed names to the two *4-Dimensional directions* (derived from the Greek language):

ANA = "upwards toward"

KATA = "downwards from"

In other explanations: this is also described as *"unfoldment"* and *"folding"*—and sometimes *"expansion"* and *"contraction"*—or even likened to a *"breath."* While it is geometrically demonstrable, it is not necessarily communicable clearly with words and descriptions that are all relative to visible *3-Dimensional* examples.

And this is not altogether different from what is implied in *"Mardukite Zuism"* with its terms (from the *Sumerian* language): *AN* and *KI.* These are the two *directions* indicated on the *Standard Model* by the *ZU-Line,* demonstrating the true *"interdimensional"* quality of *our cabala* that is not so easily depicted on paper. It *can,* however, be conceived of when applying the *"spatial exercises"* of our *Systemology.*

This subject is presented for *Wizard Level-3X* to supplement *"Intention-On-Mass"* exercises involving an *object* (such as the *ashtray*). [Review *PC-5* material on handling *"Space"* and *"Creation-Of-Space."*]

Apply the following procedure to your *Wizard Level-3X objective exercises* with an *"object."* Practice each step until there is certainty on it before proceeding to the next.

A. *Postulate* the *"Space"* around the *object* by *Intention.* Put up *eight corner-points* as a *"cube-of-space"* around the *object.* Keep this *created-space* "in place" for the remaining steps.

B. *Imagine* a *3-Dimensional* coordinate-system with three *axis* composing the *"cube."* This can be *imagined* as a *"matrix"* or a potential *"graph"* (such as you might use in a geometry class, describing an *X, Y,* and *Z-axis*). The "mathematics" behind this is unimportant. We described the *six directions* of *3-Dimensional Space* above. [These are what extend from the *three dimensional axis-lines* that are all at "right-angles" or "perpendicular" to one another.] All that is necessary for this step is that they are *realized* for what they are within the *created-space*—because the final part is: *Imagine* a *fourth dimensional axis-line* extending off both ways in *non-physical directions* (ANA and KATA; or AN and KI).

C. *Spot* the "center" of the *object.* Reach your *attention* down one *direction* of this *fourth axis-line;* and find the *object* continuing to *exist* in that *direction* until you reach the "end" of the *object.* Then *spot* the *Nothingness* on the far-side of the *object* in that *direction. Spot* the "center-point" (in the *Physical Universe*) of the *object* again. Then repeat this step in the opposite *direction,* finding the "end" of the *object* on the other side and the *Nothingness* extending beyond that.

D. Using the perception achieved from the previous steps: *Spot* a *fourth-dimensional "edge"* of the *object* extending in one of the 4-D *directions*. Alternate: *"reaching"* and *"letting-go"* of that edge with your *attention* (or by *Intention*). Then *spot* the other 4-D *"edge"* and repeat. Then alternate *"reaching"* and *"letting-go"* of *both "edges"* simultaneously. It is rather like "holding" (*sensing*) its *fourth-dimensional thickness* with *"spiritual hands."* [Once you have certainty on being able to *locate* and *perceive* its *fourth-dimensional thickness,* maintaining the *active creation* of an *axis-coordinate system* is no longer necessary.]

E. Use *Intention* to put up *eight corner-points* around the physical *object* (fairly close to it). Then, put a second set of *eight anchor-points* in the same place as the first. Take the second set and extend it out into the *fourth-dimension* until it passes beyond one of the 4-D *"edges"* of the *object,* into the *Nothingness* beyond it. Then move it back slightly so that it only encompasses the last bit of 4-D *Space* that the *object* actually occupies. Then do the same with the other *"edge."*

F. *Imagine* that the *eight corner-points* of one *cube* extend to the *eight corner-points* of the 4-D *cube.* [This is the idea behind a 4-D *"hypercube"*—or *cube within a cube*—except one of the *cubes* extends into a *fourth-dimension.*] *Imagine* that the 3-D *object* is actually in each of these *cubes* simultaneously, and also as a "smear" or "spread" stretching between them.

G. By *Intention* (or *imaginative visualization*), *get the sense* of *extending* your *"spir-*

itual hands" out and grabbing the 4-D *edges* of the *object.* Then alternate the *"Intention-based"* PCL (from the *"Change and Motion" processing* in *PC-4*):

1. *"Keep It From Going Away."*
2. *"Hold It Still."*
3. *"Make It More Solid."*

3X-D. <u>ADVANCED 3X-A</u> {3X-AX}

Refer to *"Intention: Directing Thought (Wizard Level-3X Keynote)"* for background and details on the basic *process.* It is presumed that a *Seeker* will already have practiced the basic version for a number of hours prior to handling this exercise. [Experience with procedure 3X-B and 3X-C is also required.]

3X-D combines elements from each of the three previous exercises. In this *process,* we advance the original 3X-A procedure by incorporating *Energy* along with our *Intention* for an *object* (*ashtray, &tc.*) to

"Rise Up"—similar to what is practiced in 3X-B. In addition to this, we extend our reach on the *object* into the *fourth-dimension*—as in 3X-C.

Having proficiency with the previous parts of this manual, and the high-level of *Actualized Awareness* applied by a *Seeker/Wizard* (at *Level-8*): a "shadow" of the *object's structure*—like an *"etheric"* or *"akashic"* essence of it—*will* move by applying this procedure. Whether or not the *physical object* automatically "catches up" to where you've shifted its *Beingness* to, is of course, another matter.

The degree to which a *Seeker* is at *Cause* over the *physical object* itself is likely to remain low at the beginning—therefore, we use our physical hands (as in 3X-A) to finish seeing our *intended effect* through to the end. The quotient of certainty—or percentage of *Being-at-Cause*—ebbs and flows (rises and falls) as one repeats the *process;* always end your practice on a *"win"* (when certainty is high).

We can estimate that for an individual to actually get even the smallest response from *energetic-matter* in the *Physical Universe* requires being over 90% *at-Cause* over the object/item. This is challenging to achieve in *this Physical Universe,* because the building-blocks of what is considered *"creativeness"* at a material level require a *Body* to use *effort* and *force* against *already created* (*other-determined*) *Space-Time* and *energetic-matter.* This was much less the case in much earlier (previous) versions of *Beta-Existence.*

A *Human* believes they have to use *effort* and *force* on what is *already here* in order to *do* or *have* anything. The *Space* and *mass* of *this Universe* is generally *"misowned"* by us—and therefore *persists.* Its *"Is-ness"* is really the result of an *other-determined creation;* thus we have difficulty in assuming *total responsibility* and *control* of it as being "ours." So, we go on *altering* what we have been given ("*What Is*") and making it more and more solid all the time; and ourselves becoming more *solidly fixed* on the *reality-agreements* of *this Game.*

A. Reach into the *object* and spread "*golden energy*" throughout it. Extend this *Energy* out in the *4-Dimensional* directions (see 3X-C) to fill the entire *object* with this "*golden energy*" between its *fourth-dimensional "sides."* Extend even more *Energy* into the *object's* "future" and "past" until the entirety of the *object* is filled with the "*golden energy.*" [As you continue with the remaining steps, occasionally "re-fresh" the *object* with this *Energy.*]

B. *Intend* the *object* to rise upwards. You can apply verbal commands, as in the basic version of 3X-A, or you can direct your *Intention* silently. Then "*See*" (or *Imagine/visualize*) the "etheric shadow" portion of the *object* "rise" up approximately a *foot* (*twelve inches*) above the surface (table) it is set on. If necessary, apply the 3X-C practice of also using your *"spiritual hands"* in the *fourth-dimension*; or you can apply the *"energy-beam"* method of 3X-B to improve your certainty. [Technically, the entire action is accomplished by *Intention* alone.]

C. *Acknowledge* the portion of the *object* that *did* move for having moved.

D. With the *body's hand,* move the rest of the *physical object* up to the position that you are holding the portion that moved. Have the *object "feel relieved for having caught up with itself."* Then *acknowledge* it for completing the *intended* movement.

E. *Intend* the *object* back down to where it was setting. *Acknowledge* the portion that *moves*; then use the *body's hand* to complete the action with the rest of the *physical object,* have it feel *"relieved," acknowledge* it, and *"let go"* of it.

F. Repeat STEP-B through STEP-E until an appropriate end-point.

Extended Version:

G. With eyes closed (and/or *Awareness-ejected*): perform a *"Creation-Of-Space"* (defining it with *eight corner-points, &tc.*) and *Create/Imagine* a *"Copy"* of the *object* in that *Space. Intend* the *object* to *"Rise Up"* and *"Set Down"* and have it do so, giving it *acknowledgments.*

H. Have the *object "protesting"*; and you move it anyway.

I. Have the *object "enjoying it"* as you move it.

J. Have the *object "wanting to move somewhere else"*; but you move it to where you want it anyway.

K. Alternate between *running* all of STEP-B through STEP-E and STEP-G through STEP-J repeatedly to an appropriate end-point.

3X-E. <u>BETA-INTERCONNECTEDNESS</u>

One of the *"barriers"* embedded in the

reality-agreements of *this Physical Universe* is part of what we generally refer to as *"gravity."* The underlying design for *this Universe* is "interconnectedness." By this, we mean that each manifestation or existing part of the *Space-Time Energy-Matter* of *this Universe* also acts to "hold" all the other parts in place. This is the magnitude of what a *Seeker/Wizard* is working to get greater *control* over when applying *Intention* to it—or even *ascend beyond* it (which is actually the entire point behind all of this).

[For written instruction of this exercise: we capitalize the words *"The Object"* when referring to *the object (ashtray, &tc.)* that we've been using for the *3X-series* exercises. This is important to distinguish since we will also be referring to other *"objects in the room."*]

A. *"Spot other objects in the room. For each: have (get a sense of) The Object connect with it, and disconnect from it, several times."*

B. *"Spot other objects in the room. For each: have (get a sense of) it connect with, and disconnect from, The Object, several times."*

C. *"Spot other objects in the room. For each: have (get a sense of) The Object agree with it, and disagree with it, several times."*

D. *"Spot other objects in the room. For each: have (get a sense of) it agree with, and disagree with, The Object, several times."*

E. *"Spot other objects in the room. For each: have (get a sense of) The Object communicate with it, and go out-of-communication with it, several times."*

F. *"Spot other objects in the room. For each: have (get a sense of) it communicate with, and go out-of-communication with, The Object, several times."*

G. Repeat STEP-A through F; but instead of *"objects in the room," Spot* things at a distance, including: *"The Center Of The Earth"*; *"The Center Of The Sun"*; *"The Sun (As A Mass)"*; *"The Center Of The Galaxy," &tc.*

3X-F. UNIVERSE-AS-A-TERMINAL

Practice with *getting a sense* of *The Universe* as a *terminal*. In *systematic* terms: *"gravity"* is the structural-impulse of *objects* in (and the basic design of) *this Physical Universe* to:

"keep each other from going away."

"Inertia" is the structural-impulse to:

"hold objects still."

And various built-in *mechanisms* also:

"make it more solid."

Run this *process*, *"getting the sense"* of these things to the fullest extent that you can.

A1. *"Have the Universe 'keep The Object from going away'; then have it 'let go'."* (repeat)

A2. *"Have The Object 'keep the Universe from going away'; then have it 'let go'."* (repeat)

B1. *"Have the Universe 'hold The Object completely still'; then have it 'let go and leave it uncontrolled'."* (repeat)

B2. *"Have The Object 'hold the Universe completely still'; then have it 'let go and leave it uncontrolled'."* (repeat)

C1. *"Have the Universe 'make The Object more solid'; then have it 'let go and leave it uncontrolled'."* (repeat)

C2. *"Have The Object 'make the Universe more solid'; then have it 'let go and leave it uncontrolled'."* (repeat)

3X-G. TOTAL-RESPONSIBILITY

To take total *command* and *control* of a *"creation"* (*object, &tc.*)—even a mutually "agreed-upon" *Physical Universe "creation"* (that is also being *postulated* into being by *others*; or is *other-determined*)—

the *secret* is to take *total/full responsibility* for that *"creation"* and make the *postulate* that keeps it there your own.

Run this PCL. Keep extending your *"sphere-of-responsibility"* for the *object* until it completely encompasses the *object*—*As-It-Is now, was,* and *ever will be.*

1. *"What about that object could you be responsible for?"*

   (then)

2. *"Postulate total responsibility for that object."*

   (then end that *cycle*; and repeat)

Use *concepts* from lines A1, B1, and C1 (above) to:

"Spot the structural-impulse of the Universe to ___."

A. Practice with each—*"Hold The Object Still"*; *"Keep The Object From Going Away"*; and *"Make The Object More Solid"*—in turn to get a good reality on each.

B. Practice them quickly in succession until you can fully conceive of *all three* within a *single* instantaneous *"spotting"* of *"the combined impulses being intended into the object"* by the *Universe.*

C. Repeat *getting a sense* of this *impulse;* but get it faster and faster. *Consider* it as a *"wave"* that repeats the *Intention* onto the *object* many thousand times per second. You don't have to duplicate each time-per-second individually; you simply *get a sense* of the basic *impulse* with certainty; and then *get the concept* of (or *consider*) it repeating as a super-fast *wave* that produces a *super-high frequency* (but mostly inaudible) *"hum."*

D. Then make the *wave*-frequency just a little faster until it's too fast to produce a *"hum,"* but simply *Is.* [*This* is the *"Universe Postulate"* (Alpha-Thought) of the *"Is"*-factor of the *object.*]

E. *Get a certainty* on the *Universe Postulate* (from STEP-D) and *consider* it as repeating constantly on the *object,* and *re-creating (postulating)* it into existence within consecutive *Spaces,* as though it is "carrying" the existence of the *object* "forward" in *Time.*

F. Make the *Universe Postulate* "your own"—as essentially your own *"Alpha-Thought"* or *"Postulate."* [This, itself, is accomplished by your *Intention.*] Accept *total/full responsibility* for the continuous *"re-creation"* and *"location"* of the *object* in *present-time.* Put out the *Intention: "I'm Creating It."* And have the *Universe, "acknowledge"* that.

G. *Intend* to move the *object;* and *move it.* [Use the *body's hands* if necessary.]

Scan through the processes and exercises of the *"Wizard Level-3X Procedure"* and clean up any areas that still have any *fragmentary charge,* or that you think still require significant improvement. Then work through the exercises of this *"Advanced Ability Training–3X"* section again.

This concludes the experimental portion of *Wizard Level-3*.

The remainder of this manual pertains to additional research and developments regarding *Implant-Platforms.*

IMPLANTING THE HUMAN CONDITION (*Prison Planet Implant-Platforms*)

[This discourse presents material that is not necessarily confidential, but is only appropriate for those *Seekers* that have studied (worked through) all previous *A.T. Manuals* of the *"Keys to the Kingdom"* series.]

More recent *Implants* of *this Universe*—and especially *"after Earth"* was intended as a *prison-planet*—are far more complex in their design and configuration than *older Implants* from previous *Universes.*

Since this *older* knowledge is retained by

some *universal superpower forces* (*the Implanters*) in *this Universe,* it is not surprising that *older Implants* could be combined together and expanded appropriately for more recent use. What this gives evidence for is the fact that the *"reality systems"* have become so *convoluted* and *condensed* that it has taken far greater lengths than ever before to keep an *Alpha-Spirit* suppressed within a *Universe,* or a *planet,* or the *Human Condition.*

Components of *"The Jewel"* and the original *"Heaven Incident"* during *Entry-Into-This-Universe* are far more basic than when these *Implants* are revised and revisited again later on, in relatively more recent *Implanting-Incidents.* For example: the original *Entry-Incident* uses only *one Jewel;* whereas when the same sequencing is repeated during the *Hellfire Incident* (and other more recent *incidents*), there are *three Jewels.*

The *solidarity* and *reality-agreements* of

each *descending* (*condensing*) *Universe* continued to be compounded (or superimposed) "on top" of all former ones. The *postulates* and *creations* keep "stacking up" until we are left with something as *solid* and *condensed* as *this Physical Universe.* It also seems to require layer upon layer of more complex *Implants* to keep everything existing in *this Universe* both *created* and under *control.*

What is most accessible for us to continue researching for the *Pathway*—and what is most beneficial for us to handle—is that which is specifically entrapping an *Alpha-Spirit* on *Earth,* and holding them in the *Human Condition.* Curiously, the *Implants* all stem from previous *Universes;* but they have never before been so complexly designed or so intricately interwoven into each other—or used on *Alpha-Spirits* so often.

In this manual (*AT#7*) we will provide additional data concerning *Implant-Plat-*

forms that compose, what we refer to here as, the *"Heaven Implant Series"* (since repeating the phrase *"Prison Planet Implant"* is considered rather *negative*). The *Implants* and *incidents* we treat in our work have no formal names in *human language*; nor has our *systemological data* ever been fully collected and codified within a single paradigm before now.

These new *Platforms* and *Goals-lists* represent an *incident* far more intricate than the original *Entry-Into-Universe "Heaven Incident"* and *that Goals-Sequencing*—therefore, this is *not* part of the original *Incident*, but is only intended to give the illusion of being so (and *restimulate* it). [Our earliest unpublished research on this subject referred to this series as the *"Prison Planet Implant"* so as not to confuse this research with the original *"Heaven Incident."* We could just as easily refer to this series as the *"Judgment Incident."*]

It is difficult to *"date"* the *"earliest usage"* of this *"Heaven Implant Series"* with a *GSR-Meter.* The *incident* is intentionally designed to *implant false dates,* just to make it more confusing to remember clearly (*locate* and *spot*) on the *Backtrack.* It is also difficult to determine just how often they are used for an individual's *"between-lives"* period. [To avoid *confusion, restimulation,* or *flying-by unhandled fragmentary charge*: this *Implanting* should only be handled *after* all of *Systemology Level-7* is fully *defragmented.*]

At the very least: research suggests that if an *Alpha-Spirit* is able to get nearly out of *this Solar System* (*between-lives*), there is a "net" or "screen" that seems to catch them and set them up for this *re-implanting.*

Research also indicates: use of this unique arrangement of *"Heaven Implant"* is only approximately *10,000* to *12,000* years old at most. It is specific to the *Hu-*

man Condition and *Earth* as a *prison-planet.*

We say *"Heaven Implant,"* but it is really structured like a *"court-sentencing incident."* It is the *"Judgment" archetype* (in *religion* and the *tarot*) and uses *heavy-dogmatic* symbolism that was once absent from modern religions—like *Christianity*—until its incorporation as a *restimulative control-mechanism* (against the *Human* population) during the *"Dark Ages"* of Earth's more modern history. [Most *Buddhism* seemed to escape the *effects* of this, since it already sought to avoid the *"Heaven-area"* as an *"Implant-Station."* So, our ideas about that are not really a *new consideration*.]

It has also been determined that *Implanting-Incidents* commonly incorporate IPU-*Goals* and *Symbols,* or variations thereof, in order to *restimulate* and *communicate* in an *"archetypal"* language that is universally understood—or at least includes enough recognizable content (*data*) that people will react to. [This is one reason we introduced experimental *Implant Penalty Universe* (IPU) information earlier (than what might be considered absolutely necessary) in *A.T. Manual #4.*]

The experience of actually going through these types of *incidents* is likened to an "escalator" or "treadmill." The *archetypal* scenery, or common environmental conditions, of this *Implanting-Incident* incorporates *"pyramids"* and *"aerial staircases"* and even *"spiral-like descending arrangements of pillars"* with IPU-*Goal terminals* on top of them.

The basic pattern behind the material we are going to address, originates prior to *this Universe*—but complexity has since been added to the *"command-line"* encoding for the *Platform*. The IPU data concerning *restimulative* "Price" and "Survive" *command-items* (given in *AT#4*) actually pertain to *this "Heaven Implant."*

Just as is the case with the *Hellfire Incident,* there are some individuals occupying *Human-forms* on *Earth* today that emigrated from the *Magic Universe* after the *Prison-Planet Incidents*—or have otherwise been able to side-step or escape much of the standard-issue *Human-Implanting.* However, most of the other *entities* and *fragments,* which may be affecting your case, *were* here a very long time (and are heavily *Implanted*). Like *"Platforms #1-18"* (*AT#3*), many *Implants* are researched, in part, for *releasing entities.*

An Advisement on Running Implant-Platforms: a *Seeker* may be encountering difficulties (primarily if working along the *upper-levels* of the *Pathway* without any supervision) when *processing-out Implant-Platforms,* if they are mistakenly *running* all of them the same way they treated *"The Jewel (Parts #1-5)"* in *AT#3.* That is *not* how *they* should be *run.*

Only the original *Entry-Incident "The*

Jewel" is common to all *Alpha-Spirits* of *this Universe*. It is *processed-out* completely by fully contacting each of the *command-lines until it does* give a *"Meter-read"*; and then duplicating it *"As-It-Is"* until it no longer *registers* any *charge*. **No other Implant-Platform is run that way.**

For all other *Platforms* we have provided: each *item* (*line*) is *"spotted"* and *if it does "read,"* then it is *run* until it no longer *registers* a *charge*. If the *line* doesn't *read,* then it isn't *run* any further.

If you are not able to use a *Biofeedback-Device* for your handling of *Wizard-Level* work: review the material found in *PC-11* through *PC-14,* and all *A.T. Manuals,* very thoroughly.

Being how recently this *Implanting-Incident* began being used, it is likely that an individual on *Earth* today would have at least some *fragmented charge* attached to the *Implant.*

INCIDENT SEQUENCE

This is the *incident-sequence* of being *"sentenced to Earth"*:

1. You are captured (somehow). For the original incident: it is possible that most *Humans* were part of a "rebel-fleet" against some kind of "galactic-empire" — therefore, captured *en masse* as "prisoners-of-war."

2. You are hit with *heavy energy-waves*; then told you are a *"convicted criminal"* and are awaiting sentencing for your crime. You are hit with *imprints* depicting you on trial; but you are not told what your crime is. You are told that *"memory of your horrific crime has been erased as part of this criminal rehabilitation process."*

3. Then you are sentenced in court. You are sentenced to make a copy of yourself that will be punished. You are told that after you make a copy to be punished in your place, then you will be set free. A *heavy wave-force* hits you and you sense

that you are standing beside yourself. But this is a fake *splitter-incident*; they just put up a *"doll"* that looks like you and then tell you that you have been *divided*.

4. You are told that you are the copy that is to be punished, and that they will set your real-self (the *"doll"*) free if you willingly accept your punishment.

5. You are told that you are being sentenced to *"Hell"* and they take you down into the "basement" of the courthouse, which resembles a *"Medieval-style dungeon."*

[In former *Universes*, most of the remaining sequence would have taken place in some kind of *"implant universe"* or *"pocket universe"*—or would have been used in a transition between *Universes*. But, in this case, we know that this particular *incident* is specific to *this Universe, Earth,* and *Humans*. It is more likely some kind of exceptionally advanced *electrically-implanted virtual-reality computer-simulation*. It is a *real experience,* but it does not *actually* take place within the *Physical Universe.*]

6. You are standing in the "basement" of some underground facility, at the bottom level of what they told you is *"Hell."* One of the "basement-walls" is missing, and as you look out and down you see an *"Infinite Universe"* with a vast swirling cloud of *"chaos"* suspended in the center.

7. You are told that *"you have become evil"* and that *"you have turned against your creator and therefore are to be thrown into The Chaos and be torn apart as a Spiritual Being."*

8. But then they agree to give you one last chance. They will review your history and show you how you have come to this degraded state. You are told that in doing so, they will *"run time backwards for you so that you may have another chance."* They say: *"Now pay close attention, so that you can learn from your mistakes."*

9. Then you begin to walk backwards—

literally going backwards up a staircase; occasionally down, but mostly up—working your way gradually back out of *"Hell"* and through cities and mountain-scapes, and eventually going even further and higher, backwards up a *"stairway to Heaven."*

10. As this backwards movement occurs: you are being *Implanted* with *Goals* and *command-items*. The first *Implanted-Goal* (at the bottom, while facing *Chaos*) is: TO BE ENDED. You are hit with *300 items* on this one *Goal*, as you slowly back-up the stairway.

The process is *excruciatingly* slow. The same *Platform-pattern* of *300 items* is then applied to the *next Goal* in the *sequence*, as you move a little further backwards up the stairway. This occurs in this wise for approximately *200 Goals*.

At the very top of all the stairways—there may be *six* total—you reach what they call *"Heaven"* and the *Implanted-Goal* is: TO BE CREATED (which takes place before an imprint of *God's Throne In The Clouds*).

11. At the very top, the *imprinted imagery* continues displaying various scenes of *Physical Universe "creation"* and the "creation of Humans"—much of which mirrors symbolism from the ancient *Babylonian Epic of Creation* tablets, and elements of the *Book of Genesis, &tc.* Then they tell you that everything you've seen on this backwards journey is a depiction of how you've lived your *"evil"* existence—but now you have a chance to live again, and having learned from your mistakes, will do better this time.

12. Then they "let you go"—and it's like being shot from a sling or catapult. You fly down all the staircases, getting hit with all the *Goals* and *items* again, but moving in a forward direction (and the *Goals-sequence* is experienced in reverse to how you received them moving back-

wards (going up). This all happens at an incredibly fast speed. You go all the way back to the "basement" and out the "missing wall" and start falling towards the swirling mass of clouds.

13. They catch you as you are falling. They say (something like): *"Here you've gone and done the same terrible things again. But we will give you one last chance. Now pay closer attention this time!"*

14. Then back up the staircases you go, excruciatingly slowly, getting the same *Implanted-Goals Sequencing* as you move backwards up to the top again—and back down.

15. The full sequence of "backing up the stairways" and "flying down into Chaos" occurs *three times* total. On the final (*third*) time: they allow you to fall into the *"swirling cloud of Chaos."* Once there, there are probably *millions* of *imprints* (*objects, scenery, &tc.*) that are flying around you like a tornado.

16. Then you spot a "calm area"—an "eye in the center of the hurricane" so to speak —and in the center of that "calm area" you see the *Earth.* You move down to it in order to escape the *Chaos,* and there is an overwhelming sense of *peace* and total *relief* as you go unconscious. After that, you are compelled to *reincarnate* here on *Earth.*

HEAVEN IMPLANTS (PRISON SERIES)
(*Parts #1 to 6*)

The *"Heaven Implant Series"* that occurs during the previously given *Incident-Sequence* is divided into *six* parts or *Platforms.* All *300 item-lines* occur for *each Goal;* and the individual doesn't experience the top of the *"Stairway to Heaven"* except briefly with the top/highest *Goal* in the sequence: "CREATE." In *this* section, we will provide a *short-form formula* for all *six* parts.

In the *next* section, we will provide the *Goals-list* that is used to fill in the *blank spaces* and complete this pattern-formula of *"items"* for each of the *Goals*.

Each of the *six Platforms* has its own wording-style, grammar, or syntax. We will introduce each *Platform* by explaining how the "wording" (or "tense") of a *Goal* should be modified to fit that *Platform*. That being said: the wording of the *"item-lines"* will not always sound like a conventional use of language.

PART-1

Goal is inserted {*into the blank space*} in past tense, without "TO"—for example: *"forgotten"* instead of *"to forget"*; *"ended"* instead of *"to be ended," &tc.*

1. ___
2. NOT ___
3. ABSOLUTEABLY ___
4. ABSOLUTEABLY NOT ___
5. PERFECTABLY ___

6. PERFECTABLY NOT ___
7. SUPERIORABLY ___
8. SUPERIORABLY NOT ___
9. INCOMPARABLY ___
10. INCOMPARABLY NOT ___
11. WONDERFULLABLY ___
12. WONDERFULLABLY NOT ___
13. FASCINATABLY ___
14. FASCINATABLY NOT ___
15. BEAUTIFULLABLY ___
16. BEAUTIFULLABLY NOT ___
17. HIGHLY ACCEPTABLY ___
18. HIGHLY ACCEPTABLY NOT ___
19. RECOMMENDABLY ___
20. RECOMMENDABLY NOT ___
21. ACCEPTABLY ___
22. ACCEPTABLY NOT ___
23. ENGROSSABLY ___
24. ENGROSSABLY NOT ___
25. VITALABLY ___
26. VITALABLY NOT ___
27. EAGERABLY ___
28. EAGERABLY NOT ___
29. ENTHUSIASTICABLY ___

30. ENTHUSIASTICABLY NOT ___
31. ENJOYABLY ___
32. ENJOYABLY NOT ___
33. PLEASUREABLY ___
34. PLEASUREABLY NOT ___
35. AGREEABLY ___
36. AGREEABLY NOT ___
37. DEDICATEABLY ___
38. DEDICATEABLY NOT ___
39. COMMENDABLY ___
40. COMMENDABLY NOT ___
41. DESIREABLY ___
42. DESIREABLY NOT ___
43. CREATABLY ___
44. CREATABLY NOT ___
45. WANTABLY ___
46. WANTABLY NOT ___
47. COVETABLY ___
48. COVETABLY NOT ___
49. HOPEFULABLY ___
50. HOPEFULABLY NOT ___
51. POWERFULLABLY ___
52. POWERFULLABLY NOT ___
53. DECIDEABLY ___

54. DECIDEABLY NOT ___
55. CREDITABLY ___
56. CREDITABLY NOT ___
57. DEMANDABLY ___
58. DEMANDABLY NOT ___
59. BOREABLY ___
60. BOREABLY NOT ___
61. UPSETTABLY ___
62. UPSETTABLY NOT ___
63. REGRETTABLY ___
64. REGRETTABLY NOT ___
65. DEJECTABLY ___
66. DEJECTABLY NOT ___
67. COMPULSABLY ___
68. COMPULSABLY NOT ___
69. UNSTOPABLY ___
70. UNSTOPABLY NOT ___
71. DEGRADEABLY ___
72. DEGRADEABLY NOT ___
73. IDIOTABLY ___
74. IDIOTABLY NOT ___
75. LOSEABLY ___
76. LOSEABLY NOT ___
77. BADABLY ___

78. BADABLY NOT ___
79. UNCONFRONTABLY ___
80. UNCONFRONTABLY NOT ___
81. FORGETTABLY ___
82. FORGETTABLY NOT ___
83. UNWANTABLY ___
84. UNWANTABLY NOT ___
85. PLAYABLY ___
86. PLAYABLY NOT ___
87. ABANDONABLY ___
88. ABANDONABLY NOT ___
89. ___–ING
90. NOT ___–ING
91. ___–ERS
92. NOT ___–ERS
93. ___–INGNESS
94. NOT ___–INGNESS
95. ___–ISHNESS
96. NOT ___–ISHNESS
97. ___–ATIVES
98. NOT ___–ATIVES
99. ___–IVITY
100. NOT ___–IVITY

PART-2

Goal is inserted {*into the blank space*} in present tense, with "TO"—for example: "*to forget*"; "*to be ended,*" *&tc.* [Note: some researchers got better "*Meter-reads*" without the "TO" and adding "–ING" (*forgetting, ending, &tc.*) for most of this part. Experiment with both ways to see what "*reads*" best for you.]

101. ___
102. NOT ___
103. ABSOLUTEABLE ___
104. ABSOLUTEABLE NOT ___
105. PERFECTABLE ___
106. PERFECTABLE NOT ___
107. SUPERIORABLE ___
108. SUPERIORABLE NOT ___
109. INCOMPARABLE ___
110. INCOMPARABLE NOT ___
111. WONDERFULLABLE ___
112. WONDERFULLABLE NOT ___
113. FASCINATABLE ___
114. FASCINATABLE NOT ___

115. BEAUTIFULLABLE ___
116. BEAUTIFULLABLE NOT ___
117. HIGHLY ACCEPTABLE ___
118. HIGHLY ACCEPTABLE NOT ___
119. RECOMMENDABLE ___
120. RECOMMENDABLE NOT ___
121. ACCEPTABLE ___
122. ACCEPTABLE NOT ___
123. ENGROSSABLE ___
124. ENGROSSABLE NOT ___
125. VITALABLE ___
126. VITALABLE NOT ___
127. EAGERABLE ___
128. EAGERABLE NOT ___
129. ENTHUSIASTICABLE ___
130. ENTHUSIASTICABLE NOT ___
131. ENJOYABLE ___
132. ENJOYABLE NOT ___
133. PLEASUREABLE ___
134. PLEASUREABLE NOT ___
135. AGREEABLE ___
136. AGREEABLE NOT ___
137. DEDICATEABLE ___
138. DEDICATEABLE NOT ___

139. COMMENDABLE ___
140. COMMENDABLE NOT ___
141. DESIREABLE ___
142. DESIREABLE NOT ___
143. CREATABLE ___
144. CREATABLE NOT ___
145. WANTABLE ___
146. WANTABLE NOT ___
147. COVETABLE ___
148. COVETABLE NOT ___
149. HOPEFULABLE ___
150. HOPEFULABLE NOT ___
151. POWERFULLABLE ___
152. POWERFULLABLE NOT ___
153. DECIDEABLE ___
154. DECIDEABLE NOT ___
155. CREDITABLE ___
156. CREDITABLE NOT ___
157. DEMANDABLE ___
158. DEMANDABLE NOT ___
159. BOREABLE ___
160. BOREABLE NOT ___
161. UPSETTABLE ___
162. UPSETTABLE NOT ___

163. REGRETTABLE ___
164. REGRETTABLE NOT ___
165. DEJECTABLE ___
166. DEJECTABLE NOT ___
167. COMPULSABLE ___
168. COMPULSABLE NOT ___
169. UNSTOPABLE ___
170. UNSTOPABLE NOT ___
171. DEGRADEABLE ___
172. DEGRADEABLE NOT ___
173. IDIOTABLE ___
174. IDIOTABLE NOT ___
175. LOSEABLE ___
176. LOSEABLE NOT ___
177. BADABLE ___
178. BADABLE NOT ___
179. UNCONFRONTABLE ___
180. UNCONFRONTABLE NOT ___
181. FORGETTABLE ___
182. FORGETTABLE NOT ___
183. UNWANTABLE ___
184. UNWANTABLE NOT ___
185. PLAYABLE ___
186. PLAYABLE NOT ___

187. ABANDONABLE ___
188. ABANDONABLE NOT ___
189. (TO) ___–ING
190. NOT ___–ING
191. (TO) ___–ERS
192. NOT ___–ERS
193. (TO) ___–INGNESS
194. NOT ___–INGNESS
195. (TO) ___–ISHNESS
196. NOT ___–ISHNESS
197. (TO) ___–ATIVES
198. NOT ___–ATIVES
199. (TO) ___–IVITY
200. NOT ___–IVITY

PART-3

Goal is inserted {*into the blank space*} in present-tense, without "TO"—for example: *"forget"*; *"being ended,"* *&tc.*

201. ___
202. NOT ___
203. ___–ING
204. NOT ___–ING

205. ___–ERS
206. NOT ___–ERS
207. ___–INGNESS
208. NOT ___–INGNESS
209. ___–ISHNESS
210. NOT ___–ISHNESS
211. ___–ATIVES
212. NOT ___–ATIVES
213. ___–IVITY
214. NOT ___–IVITY

PART-4

Goal is inserted {*into the blank space*} without "TO" and as an "–ING" form; "*to forget*" becomes "*forgetting.*" On the "TO BE" type *Goals,* the "–ING" is added to "BE"; "*to be ended*" becomes "*being ended.*"

215. THOSE WHO ARE ___
216. THOSE WHO ARE NOT ___
217. GOALS THAT LEAD TO ___
218. THOSE WHO HATE ___
219. ACTIVELY ___

220. DOESN'T WANT TO BE ___
221. ADVANTAGES OF ___
222. NO ADVANTAGES OF ___
223. ANY NECESSITY FOR ___
224. NO NECESSITY FOR ___
225. ANY EXISTENCE OF ___
226. SUPPRESSING EXISTENCE OF ___
227. ANY INSTANCE ON ___
228. INVALIDATING ___
229. ANY DEPENDENCE ON ___
230. DENYING ___
231. THOSE WHO ARE CREATING ___
232. THOSE WHO ARE DESTROYING ___
233. ANY ACTIONS OF ___
234. NO ACTIONS OF ___
235. ANY BELIEF IN ___
236. NO BELIEF IN ___
237. PROPONENTS OF ___
238. OPPONENTS OF ___
239. FANTASTIC IMPORTANCE OF ___
240. UNIMPORTANCE OF ___
241. OBSESSIONS FOR ___

242. REPULSIONS FOR ___
243. INTERESTINGNESS OF ___
244. UNINTERESTINGNESS OF ___
245. CONCERNS OF ___
246. NO CONCERNS OF ___
247. UPSETS ABOUT ___
248. NO UPSETS ABOUT ___
249. DESPERATIONS OF ___
250. NO DESPERATIONS OF ___
251. FRENZIEDNESS(ES) OF ___
252. NO FRENZIEDNESS(ES) OF ___
253. PAINFULLNESS OF ___
254. PAINLESSNESS OF ___
255. HOPELESSNESS OF ___
256. HOPEFULLNESS OF ___

PART-5

For the "odd numbered" *items,* the *Goal* continues to be inserted in present-tense without "TO" and as an "–ING" form; *"forgetting," &tc.* For "TO BE" type *Goals,* the "–ING" is added to the "BE"; *"to be ended"* becomes *"being ended."*

The "even numbered" *items* are stated as a *Beingness.* In this case, for the "TO BE" type *Goals,* the "TO BE" is simply dropped; *"to be ended"* becomes *"(an) ended (being)."*

257. THE EXHAUSTIONS OF ___
258. AN EXHAUSTED ___ BEING
259. THE STUPIDITY OF ___
260. A STUPIDIFIED ___ BEING
261. THE EFFORTS OF ___
262. A WEAKENED ___ BEING
263. THE UNREWARDINGNESS OF ___
264. AN UNREWARDED ___ BEING
265. THE COMPLICATIONS OF ___
266. A COMPLICATED ___ BEING
267. THE DEMANDS OF ___
268. A DEMANDING ___ BEING
269. THE DETERMINATIONS OF ___
270. A DETERMINED ___ BEING
271. THE FOOLISHNESS OF ___
272. A FOOLISH ___ BEING
273. THE COMPULSIONS OF ___
274. A COMPULSIVE ___ BEING

275. THE INVALIDATIONS OF ___
276. AN INVALIDATED ___ BEING
277. THE LIMITATIONS OF ___
278. A LIMITED ___ BEING
279. THE DEGRADATIONS OF ___
280. A DEGRADED ___ BEING
281. THE OVERWHELMS OF ___
282. AN OVERWHELMED ___ BEING
283. THE MISERY OF ___
284. A MISERABLE ___ BEING
285. THE UNAWARENESS OF ___
286. AN UNAWARE ___ BEING
287. THE OPPONENTS OF ___
288. AN OPPOSED ___ BEING

PART-6

For the "odd numbered" *items*, the *Goal* continues to be inserted in present-tense without "TO" and as an "–ING" form; *"forgetting," &tc.* For "TO BE" type *Goals*, the "–ING" is added to the "BE"; *"to be ended"* becomes *"being ended."*

The "even numbered" *items* are stated in

the basic "TO {GOAL}" style; *"to forget," "to be ended," &tc.*

The last *item-line* links the *Platform* to the *next Goal* in the *sequence.* This last *item-line* is actually a *"negation-item"* (or *"op-positional nix-item"*) of the *next Goal.* It immediately precedes the first *item-line* of PART-1 for the *next Goal.*

[Note that unlike the original *"Heaven Incident"* pageantry of *Goals-Sequencing,* this entire *Implanting-Incident* runs the *sequence-ordering* in each direction (*three times*), and the *"next Goal"* depends on whether you are going "ascending" or "descending" on the *chain.*]

289. THE FORBIDDENNESS OF ___
290. SOMEBODY WHO NEEDS ___
291. A HATRED OF ___
292. SOMEBODY WHO LOVES ___
293. THE INHIBITEDNESS OF ___
294. SOMEBODY WHO DESIRES ___
295. THE ABSENCE OF ___

296. SOMEBODY WHO COMPULSIVELY CREATES ___
297. STOPPED ___
298. SOMEBODY WITH THE GOAL ___
299. ANY IMPOSSIBILITIES OF ___
300. SOMEONE OR SOMETHING WITH THE GOAL ___
301. THE NON-EXISTENCE OF ___
302. THE GOAL ___
303. {*current goal*}
304. NOT {*next goal*}

HEAVEN IMPLANTS (PRISON SERIES)
(*Goal-Sequencing List*)

This is the *Goal-Sequencing List* in the order that it is first encountered in the *Implanting-Incident.*

On your first *run* through the *sequence,* you are working from the "bottom" to the "top." You begin at the "bottom" and walk "up" a *stairway* backwards while perceiving *300 items* for that *Goal.* The remaining *stairway* extends upward *behind* you. The "bottom-level" *Goal* is: TO BE ENDED.

There is usually some type of unique related *imprinted-imagery* that is displayed for each *Goal* while the *items* are *Implanted.* We have very limited data to describe this (given with each *Goal* when available). The scenery from *one Goal* "scrolls" or "blends" into the scenery of whatever is *next* without any "break."

On your second *run* through the *sequence,* you will treat the *Goals-list* in the reverse order of what is printed here. For this, you will work from the "top" and proceed forward going "down" the stairway. The "top-level" *Goal* is: TO BE CREATED.

We have certainty on the actual *Incident-Sequence,* the *first* and *last* primary *Goal* for the *Goal-Sequence,* and an estimated 80-90% of the *Goals* that lie between. Based on our experience, this is apparently sufficient enough *data* to "*Spot*" in order to *defragment* the entire *Platform-series.*

1. TO BE ENDED
   A black pathway through empty space, ending at the swirling spiral of Chaos.
2. TO BE TORTURED
   A dark dungeon; layered down to the "final pit" and a pathway through Nothingness.
3. TO BE INSUBSTANTIAL
4. TO BE FLAYED
   Strapped down to a stretcher; being wheeled into surgery.
5. TO BE NUMB
   An ice-cave; crystalline arches at the entrance.
6. TO BE FROZEN
   Snow-covered landscape; ice-sculptures (statues) say the items. On Part-6, you are dunked in ice-water on each item.
7. TO BE BURNED
   Burning landscape; flames say the items.

Repeatedly dropped into a "fiery pit" (on each item).

8. TO BE UNAFFECTED

   Surrounded by violent explosions that don't quite hit you.

9. TO BE HORRIFIED

   Smokey pits; victims on either side of the stairway; demons say the items.

10. TO BE UNAWARE

11. TO BE IN HELL

    Bridges over flames and rivers of fire. Bridges lead to cities; final bridge leads to mountain-cave.

12. TO BE GAMELESS

    Gray pathway near mountain-cave; gray clouds; color washed-out of everything.

13. TO BE HAUNTED

    Gray landscape.

14. TO BE SELF-PITYING

    Rough-rock bridges over ash.

15. TO BE DRAINED

    Bleak gray landscape with dark

misshapen trees. Spirits hit at you and it feels like they pull away energy.

16. TO BE IGNITED
17. TO BE INTERIORIZED

    Snapping into dead bodies, one to another, in a morgue.
18. TO BE BODILESS

    Floating over a pile of ashes. Nice things are all around but you can't grab a hold of them.
19. TO BE BURIED
20. TO BE MOURNFUL

    Walking through a graveyard; tombstones say items.
21. TO BE NON-EXISTENT
22. TO BE DEAD
23. TO FAIL

    Walking through a battlefield with barbed-wire fences. Fence-poles say items.
24. TO BE WIPED OUT

    Battlefield; dying soldiers say items.

25. TO BE APATHETIC
Pathway through war-torn battlefield.

26. TO BE DEFEATED
Battlefield. Tanks and planes say "odd-numbered" items; fighting soldiers say "even-numbered" items.

27. TO BE MURDEROUS
Walking along a tall wall overlooking battlefield; exploding bombs say the items.

28. TO BE HATED
In a railroad car, on a track running between barbed-wire fences of battlefield.

29. TO BE IGNORED
On railroad car.

30. TO BE BLAMED
On railroad car; billboards say items.

31. TO BE UNCARING
Elegant railroad car; passing people starving and pleading for help.

32. TO BE POSSESSED (TAKEN OVER)
Railway train shed; loud-speakers say items.

33. TO BE VENGEFUL

Between a train shed and a harbor.

34. TO BE PERSECUTED

Running alongside a harbor near a village, trying to escape townspeople with pitchforks, &tc., who say the items.

35. TO BE PARANOID

Floating in dark waters.

36. TO BE PURPOSELESS

A canal. Poles in water say items.

37. TO BE SELF-CONFLICTING

Canal with cottages along the banks. You try to go in different directions simultaneously. You split/divide on the "odd-numbered" items, and recombine on the "even-numbered" items.

38. TO BE COMBINED

Body is on a pole of the canal near cottages. Copies of yourself come flying out of cottages and snap-in to your body.

39. TO BE DIVIDED

Canal boat. Floating past docks during

electrical storm. Copies of yourself are standing at edge of docks, then turn around when you approach and walk away. Lightning bolts say items.

40. TO BE UNCHANGING

    Canal.

41. TO BE SICK

    Canal; lying sick in boat.

42. TO BE HOPELESS

    Canal; sidewalk to either side; statues say items.

43. TO BE SELF-INVALIDATIVE

    Canal.

44. TO GIVE UP

    Canal through a desert. Pyramids, on either side, say items.

45. TO FEEL MISERABLE

    Amusement park ride; inside some kind of box that jerks around.

    {might be missing *Goals* here}

46. TO BE UNCONSCIOUS

47. TO BE HURT

In a cart/car; going down a steep mountain; smashing into things.

48. TO BE SELF-DESTRUCTIVE

Pits containing various hazards line both sides of the roadway. The pits say the items. On the "odd-numbered" items, you step off the roadway and fall into a pit. On the "even-numbered" items, you end up back on the roadway.

49. TO BE TRAPPED

Amusement park; carousel; going up and down on a pole; fake horses all around.

50. TO BE LOST

"Spinning plates" (?)

51. TO BE LOCATED

Walking down streets; walking down corridors. Doors (with faces) say items.

52. TO BE DISPERSED

Strapped to a bulls-eye on a flying target; things keep hitting you. On the "odd-numbered" items, pieces of the body fly off in all directions. On the "even-

numbered" items, the pieces are pulled back together.

53. TO BE OVERWHELMED
    Amusement park. Contains imagery from other parts of the Implanting-Incident.
54. TO BE PUNISHED
    Amusement park.
55. TO BE DOMINEERING
    Amusement park.
56. TO BE CRIPPLED
    Amusement park.
57. TO BE SPINNING
    Amusement park; spinning pole.
58. TO BE STOPPED
    Amusement park; ride-car keeps stopping in unpleasant places.
59. TO BE DIZZY (?)
60. TO BE UNAFFECTED (?)
61. TO BE UNBALANCED
    Amusement park; "spinning plates" (?)

{might be missing *Goals* here}

62. TO BE CARELESS
63. TO BE SELF-CONTROLLED
64. TO BE RECKLESS
65. TO BE CONTROLLED (?)
66. TO BE GET WORSE
    Underground cave. Stalagmites say "odd-numbered" items; the floor says "even-numbered" items.
67. TO BE DRUGGED (?)
68. TO BE AGONIZED (?)
69. TO EXPERIENCE NOTHING
70. TO BE ELECTROCUTED
    Hitting against large round electrified terminals on either side. (Like being in a pinball game.)

    {might be missing *Goals* here}

71. TO BE DISMEMBERED (?)
72. TO BE WORRIED (?)
73. TO BE UNTHINKING
    In a swamp; on a boat.
74. TO BE DEPRESSED

Poling a boat through a muddy swamp.

75. TO BE INDIFFERENT

    Being dragged through a muddy swamp by snakes (that say the items).

76. TO BE STUCK

    Hopping through a muddy tar-swamp. You get stuck on the "odd-numbered" items, and lift out on the "even-numbered" items.

77. TO BE FLEEING

    Wading through muddy swamp in haste.

78. TO BE INFESTED

    In a marsh, on a raft. Firefly-like bugs enter your body on the "odd-numbered" items. Feeling of being infested with entities.

{might be missing *Goals* here}

79. TO BE EVIL (?)

    Creatures rise up out of marshy swamp to say items.

80. TO BE UNIMPORTANT

    Walking through marsh; stakes sticking

up out of the water with heads on them, which say the items. There are electric shocks associated with the "odd-numbered" items.

81. TO BE IMPLANTED
82. TO BE VISCOUS

    On a cliffside, near the sea; stairway leads down into the water.
83. TO BE PURSUED

    Running through a forest toward a beach.
84. TO BE NERVOUS

    In the forest; trees say the items.
85. TO BE CRIMINAL

    Walking down urban streets.
86. TO BE DOCILE
87. TO BE TREATED

    Hospital.
88. TO BE INSANE

    Hospital.
89. TO BE CONDEMNED

    Walking from a courthouse to jail;

prisoners say items.

90. TO BE DISHONEST
91. TO BE ACCUSED

    Walking between pillars (that say items).
92. TO BE GUILT-RIDDEN

    In a forest; faces on trees say items.
93. TO BE TREASONOUS
94. TO BE BLINDED
95. TO BE SPYING
96. TO BE BETRAYED

    {might be missing *Goals* here}
97. TO BE VILIFIED (?)
98. TO BE TREACHEROUS (?)
99. TO BE DEGRADED
100. TO BE ASHAMED
101. TO BE PERVERTED

     Carnival. (?)
102. TO HAVE CRAVINGS

     Carnival market; things on display. (?)
103. TO BE EMPTY

     Floating above market or shopping mall.

104. TO BE GLUTTONOUS

Restaurant terrace overlooking market or shopping mall.

105. TO BE REJECTED

A mall-tunnel or concourse.

106. TO BE DISGUSTING

A sewer-like subway station/tunnel.

107. TO BE TIDY

A carpeted hallway.

108. TO BE MESSY

109. TO BE CLUNG-TO

110. TO BE ABANDONED

111. TO BE DEPENDENT

112. TO BE UNFEELING

113. TO BE SEXUAL

114. TO BE ALONE

115. TO BE TOGETHER

116. TO BE ISOLATED

117. TO BE CORRUPTING

118. TO BE CORRUPTED

119. TO BE INHIBITED

120. TO BE WANTON

121. TO BE FRUSTRATED

{might be missing a *Goal* here}

122. TO BE DISINTERESTED

123. TO BE DISAPPOINTED

124. TO BE HUMAN

Goal might actually be: To Be Selfish. (Or "To Be Selfish" might need to be inserted as next goal or previous goal.)

{might be missing a *Goal* here}

125. TO BE ENRAGED

126. TO BE DROPPED

127. TO BE CARRIED

On a ski-lift. (?)

128. TO BE EXHAUSTED

Trudging up a mountain-slope from a beach; eventually reaching snowy area.

129. TO BE OVEREXERTED

{might be missing a *Goal* here}

130. TO HALLUCINATE

131. TO BE TERRIFIED

132. TO BE FOOLISH

133. TO BE RESPONSIBLE

Traveling in a car at high speed, down a steep slope. Light-posts say items as you pass by.

134. TO BE IRRESPONSIBLE

135. TO BE BURDENED

Trudging through primitive village carrying many things.

136. TO BE NEGLIGENT

137. TO BE CAREFUL

138. TO BE CRUSHED

Industrial factory-like environment; on a conveyer-belt. Cylinders come down and crush you; walls smash inward from the side.

139. TO BE INATTENTIVE

140. TO BE SELF-CRITICAL

{might be missing *Goals* here}

141. TO BE REGRETFUL

142. TO BE INCOMPETENT

143. TO BE ENSLAVED

144. TO BE CRUEL

145. TO BE IRRITATED (?)

146. TO BE EXPLOITED (?)

147. TO BE RESISTED (?)

148. TO BE MISLED (?)

149. TO BE ASLEEP

Fluffy pillow-like landscape; soft pathway; stuffed-animals, on either side, say the items.

150. TO BE TIRED

{might be missing *Goals* here}

151. TO BE CRITICAL

152. TO BE CRITICIZED

Broad stairway in the air; statues along either side say the items.

153. TO BE ARROGANT

Roadway in the sky.

154. TO BE WRONG

155. TO BE IMPORTANT

Roadway in the sky. "Pennant-poles" say the items.

156. TO BE BOTHERED

157. TO BE POWERFUL
158. TO BE TROUBLED
159. TO HAVE PICTURES
160. TO BE UNSEEING
161. TO BE REVOLTED
162. TO BE AFFECTED
163. TO BE TOUGH (?)
164. TO BE FRAGILE (?)
165. TO HAVE NOTHING
166. TO BE POSSESSIVE
167. TO BE MASSLESS
    Moving through "solid" doors.
168. TO BE SOLID
    Walking beneath iron-arches.
169. TO BE ALTERED (?)
170. TO BE INCOMPLETE (?)
171. TO BE BLOCKED (?)
172. TO BE IRRADIATED (?)
173. TO BE DISTRACTED (?)
174. TO FORGET
175. TO REGRET

176. TO LEVITATE

Walking on a transparent bridge in the sky. All of the imagery is of harmful-acts.

177. TO COMPULSIVELY CREATE

Aerial stairway.

178. TO BE CAST OUT

Thrown out of heaven, through its gates.

179. TO BE IN HEAVEN

Pathway through clouds between the gates and the heavenly kingdom.

180. TO BE REBELLIOUS

181. TO BE GOOD

You eventually back up all the way to where "God's Throne" sits at the top of the stairway.

182. TO BE CREATED

The top-most item displays you being created by "God."

HEAVEN IMPLANTS (ETHICS SERIES) (*Implant-Running Process / Goals-List*)

When an *Alpha-Spirit* first separates from the *Infinity of Nothingness,* it is an incredibly powerful—but also an incredibly innocent and naïve—*Spiritual Being* with a *creative* nature. The one thing we could absolutely say for certain is: the basic nature of the *Alpha-Spirit* is definitely *not* "inherently evil."

There is a long history of attempts to *Implant* individuals to "make them good." Of course, the only reason they do the things they do is because of how *fragmented* they are; and one of the reasons individuals have become so *fragmented,* is the tremendous quantity of accumulated *Implants* they've been subjected to.

Implanting has never once "made someone good." For one thing: an individual doesn't need to be "made to be good." *Ethics* have never been successfully *"enforced"* and *"personally developed"* simultaneously.

An individual either *has* the *Awareness* and *ability-to-confront* what has happened (and *decide* to *change* their course of future *thought* and *action*), or they *don't* have the *Awareness*—in which case, they are not able to see what has happened *"As-It-Is,"* and/or their *considerations* are too heavily wrapped up in *justification*. In any case: *Implanting* will not make the individual *more aware*.

There have been many versions of the *"Ethics-Implant"* pattern, extending back through several *Universes*. In each *Universe*, the *Platform-pattern* tends to become a little more complex, with more *command-lines* added to the existing *Platform* from a prior *Universe*—as is commonly found in later (more recent) *Implants*.

The real purpose behind any *Implant* is to suppress *Alpha-Spirits,* reduce their *Actualized Awareness,* and keep them under some kind of *"other-determined"* (rather than *"Self-determined"*) *control.* You can *"condition"* individuals into being quiet, complacent, orderly *"good citizens"*—but this doesn't make them more *ethical.*

An *"Ethics-Implant"* isn't only about making the *Implanted*-individual a more ethical person; it sells them on the idea that "everyone is *bad*" and that this is "what is *wrong* with everyone" (*including* themselves), and that "everyone needs to have *ethics enforced* on them." It gets one to be more tolerant/agreeable to *enforcement.*

We include this as part of the *"Heaven Implants"* because it tends to show up *between-lives* and emphasizes what some might consider *"religious morality"* (although it really serves a more "civic/ societal" function). In contrast to many other *Implants,* the *"items"* of an *Ethics-Platform* all seem "positive" or "good things"—such as *"creating goodness"* and *"destroying criminality."* But, this deceptively just makes the person more agreeable to the general content/message of the *Implant,* which again, is inhibiting *"thinking for one's self."*

Due to the many variations and versions, critical research-time was not spent in developing full *Platforms* that are each only slightly modified from one another. The *Goals-list* for this *Implant* is also *not* so deeply ingrained or heavily charged that we have to run hundreds of *items* off of a *Goal* in order to *defragment* it.

Therefore, we provide an *"Ethics-Implant Running Procedure."* It is designed to only apply as many details as are necessary to be able to easily *"defrag-by-realization"* (by *Spotting* a few key aspects of the *Platforms*). This procedure only has a dozen steps; and is *run* on each of *20 Goals* (as given in the attached *Goals-list*).

IMPLANT-RUNNING PROCEDURE

A. *Spot* the first *item* of the original *Implant-Platform* as used in the *Symbols Universe*:

TO BE {*Goal*} IS NATIVE STATE

B. *Spot* the first *item* of the *Implant-Platform* as used in a later version:

TO CREATE {*Positive State*} IS NATIVE STATE

C. *Spot* the *item* related to the later *Implant-Platform* from STEP-B:

TO DESTROY {*Negative State*} IS NATIVE STATE

D. Another version uses the entire series of *64 Implanted Penalty-Universe* (IPU) *Goals; running* from *"Create"* to *"Endure."* You should only need to *Spot* a few of them. The first two and last two of the series are given below to demonstrate the *pattern*. [Refer to *AT#4* for additional IPU details (if needed).]

TO BE IS TO CREATE {*Positive State*}

TO BE IS TO CAUSE {*Positive State*}

TO BE IS TO EAT/ABSORB {*Positive State*}

TO BE IS TO ENDURE (ANYTHING FOR THE SAKE OF) {*Positive State*}

E. As related to the version from STEP-D: this *Implant-Platform* uses *64 inverted IPU-Goals* in *reverse order*—from *"Endure"* (now inverted as *"Dissipate"*) up to *"Create"* (now inverted as *"Destroy"*). These are run on the *"Negative Goal States"* (as given in the *Goals-list*). You should only need to *Spot* a few of them. The first two and last two of the series are given below to demonstrate the *inverted reverse-order pattern*.

TO BE IS TO DISSIPATE {*Negative State*}

TO BE IS TO REFUSE {*Negative State*}

TO BE IS TO UNDO {*Negative State*}

F. The earliest versions included a *"splitter-incident."* In this case, you were required to push *fragments* of yourself onto others to "make them follow the rules." [Refer to *AT#5* concerning *"Control Entities"* (CE).]

1. *"Spot pushing fragments of yourself onto others and compelling them to be {positive state}."*
2. *"Spot pushing fragments of yourself onto others and inhibiting them from {negative state}."*

Note: any *fragments* (*split pieces*) you *Spot,* you should *run* the *"Entity Locational Procedure"* (*AT#5*) on them (*"Point to the being you divided from"*).

Also (if necessary or applicable): handle any more recent actions of *"forcing others to be { positive state }"* and/or *"inhibiting others from { negative state }."* [In this case, we don't mean reasonable efforts to help others improve; we mean more heavy-handed scenarios.]

G. *Spot* any *entities* (or *fragments*) that have been pushed onto you (by others) to compel you *"to be { positive state}"* or *"inhibit you from { negative state}."* Handle by having the *entity "Spot"* the false data of the *Implant* and/or the *top item* (STEP-A); or else, *"Locational Procedure," &tc*. [See *AT#5*.]

H. *Defragment* some of the *tendencies/considerations* laid in by the *Implant.*

1. *"Spot wanting to be compelled by others to be {positive state}."*
2. *"Spot wanting to be inhibited by others from {negative state}."*
3. *"Spot the realization that these cravings/tendencies were installed by the Implant."*

I. *Defragment* some of the *Implanted data.*

"Spot the false data: that people are basically {negative state}."

J. *Defragment* some misconceptions.

"Spot the misconception: that this Implant is necessary to your well-being, and the well-being of others."

K. *Spot* the first *item* of the *IPU-Platform. Spot* this for yourself—and for any partially awake *entities* that haven't *released/dispersed* yet.

TO CREATE IS NATIVE STATE

L. (If necessary) *Spot* the first *item* of the *Agreements Universe-Platform. Spot* this for yourself—and for any partially awake *entities* that haven't *released/dispersed* yet.

TO AGREE IS NATIVE STATE

[Note that if you don't get a sense of relief on the *Goal-item* from this procedure: *spot* any *harmful-acts* on the *Backtrack* regarding your participation in designing the *Implant*; or *Implanting* others; or wanting others *Implanted* with this; or even forcing others to be *Implanted* with this.]

ETHICS-IMPLANT GOAL-LIST

There are *20 Implanted Goal-items* for this *Platform-pattern*. The basic *Goal* is listed in capital letters. There are also "Create" (*positive state*) and "Destroy" (*negative state*) *Goal-items* listed for each basic *Goal*. Use this data to fill-in {indicated spaces} for the steps of the procedure. You may have to slightly adjust the wording of a *goal-state* to make sense in the *processing command-lines* of the procedure.

1. TO BE ETHICAL
   POS. (to create) ethics
   NEG. (to destroy) criminality
2. TO BE RESOURCEFUL
   POS. (to create) resourcefulness
   NEG. (to destroy) complacency
3. TO BE SYMPATHETIC
   POS. (to create) sympathy
   NEG. (to destroy) callousness
4. TO BE DUTIFUL
   POS. (to create) dutifulness

NEG. (to destroy) carelessness

5. TO BE RESPONSIBLE
   POS. (to create) responsibility
   NEG. (to destroy) irresponsibility
6. TO BE HONORABLE
   POS. (to create) honor
   NEG. (to destroy) dishonor
7. TO BE LOYAL
   POS. (to create) loyalty
   NEG. (to destroy) disloyalty
8. TO BE TRUSTWORTHY
   POS. (to create) trustworthiness
   NEG. (to destroy) betrayal
9. TO BE INDUSTRIOUS
   POS. (to create) industriousness
   NEG. (to destroy) laziness
10. TO BE MERCIFUL
    POS. (to create) mercifulness
    NEG. (to destroy) vengefulness
11. TO BE OBEDIENT
    POS. (to create) obedience

NEG. (to destroy) disobedience

12. TO BE PATIENT
    POS. (to create) patience
    NEG. (to destroy) impatience
13. TO BE HELPFUL
    POS. (to create) helpfulness
    NEG. (to destroy) unhelpfulness
14. TO BE CARING
    POS. (to create) caring
    NEG. (to destroy) uncaring
15. TO BE PROTECTIVE
    POS. (to create) protectiveness
    NEG. (to destroy) unprotectiveness
16. TO BE THRIFTY
    POS. (to create) thriftiness
    NEG. (to destroy) wastefulness
17. TO BE POLITE
    POS. (to create) politeness
    NEG. (to destroy) rudeness
18. TO BE RESPECTFUL
    POS. (to create) respectfullness

NEG. (to destroy) disrespectfullness

19. TO BE GOOD
    POS. (to create) goodness
    NEG. (to destroy) badness

20. TO BE REVERENT
    POS. (to create) reverence
    NEG. (to destroy) irreverence

SPIRITUAL-DISABILITY IMPLANT
Experimental Ascension Processing

[This is *experimental* material. It has been researched and developed sufficiently for effective use and therefore is included with *Wizard Level-3* procedures. Slight revisions may occur in the future where noted and/or it may be reclassified for a higher *Wizard-Level*.]

This *Implant-Platform* is *very old*—likely originating in the *"Symbols Universe"* (see

AT#1) or possibly earlier. Unlike relatively more recently designed *Implants,* the *effectiveness* of this one is not the result of *non-sensical confusion*. It was carefully constructed to *"imitate"*—and be *experienced as*—an individual's *own thoughts.*

When first researched, we referred to this *Implant* as a *"mental-disability" Implant* (but such terminology is commonly misunderstood to mean something else regarding the *Human Condition*). We originally labeled it for the *"Mind"* because it *fixes "mental-circuitry" in-place* for many *considerations* that an *Alpha-Spirit* would have otherwise treated (or not) on their own *Self-determination* (*knowingly/consciously* with *Alpha-Thought*).

It covertly installs "foundations" for a *fragmented Mind*—establishing *"circuitry"* (or *associative connections*) with various *concepts, considerations,* and *terminals;* none of which seems, on the surface, as though it is "damaging." But it is; because it reduces *spiritual ability* by *fixing attention* (as *fragmentary charge*) on a lot of *considerations*.

Each *series-run* of the *Implant* is modified by a single basic *Intention* or *Goal*. The *first three series-runs* draw an individual "in" to the content by using "I.." statements. This means it starts by having hundreds of "I.." statements *firing* "internally" as though they were one's own. The remainder of the *series-runs* concern "To (do something)" statements, worded as *associative-knowledge* about basic *Goals*.

At this point in *Advanced Training*, it should already be fairly obvious as to "why" *compulsively* and *unknowingly* maintaining *fragmentary charge* on all of these *"items"* is *spiritually unhealthy* or *debilitating*. Therefore, let us focus on the mechanics of the *Implant* itself, and *defragmenting* the *Platform*.

To illustrate this: let's take up a *"null-example"* (that does not actually appear in the *Implant-Platform*) about *"Eating."* It probably would be included if this *Implant* were constructed today, but at the time of its origination, "food-intake" *considerations* were not a "standard" part of an *Alpha-Spirit's* existence or reality.

A basic short-form formula for this *Implant-Platform* would only include the main reoccurring *"root"* for each *"item-line."* In this case:

`0.1.X` ____ TO EAT
`0.2.X` ____ TO STARVE

Here you see what appear to be opposing *concepts*. All of the *items* in this *Implant* occur in pairs. Each *series* inserts a different *keyword* or *impulse* at the start of the statement. The first statement is given a "positive" and the second is given a "negative." And in the end, they both will basically mean the same thing. For the first *series-run* of *"I want"/"I don't want,"* the *command-lines* would be *processed-out* (*discharged/defragged*) as:

```
0.1.1  (I WANT) TO EAT
0.2.1  (I DON'T WANT) TO STARVE
```

At first glance, it would seem like there is nothing wrong with these *considerations.* But, what if you had never had them before? What if there was no need to even *consider* them?—but here they are: the formation of a specific *"thought-tendency"* or *"circuit"* about *eating, food, &tc.* Once the *"wanting"* is installed, it's that much easier to install a *"need"* on that *"circuit"* for the *second series-run,* when the *command-lines* change to:

```
0.1.2  (I NEED) TO EAT
0.2.2  (I CAN'T BEAR) TO STARVE
```

By starting at the "top" (earliest point) of the *Implant-Platform,* the heavier laden *charge* can be *dispersed* from the foundations before the additional *series-runs.* Although there were originally over a hundred *series-runs* during the original

Implanting-Incident, the entire *pattern* is likely to start coming apart and *disperse* after *processing-out* only a few dozen (for a *Wizard Level-3* practitioner) when working from the "top."

After the *first three series-runs,* the remainder of the *Implant* contains many arbitrary *considerations* that add even more *"energetic-mass"* to all those key areas that were just installed. They are really *"equations"* of *"associative thought."* The *command-items* all relay that "one thing *is* (equal to) another thing"—and this is done thousands of times over the course of the remaining series-runs.

To illustrate how the remaining *series* are *run,* we will apply the *"fourth series-run"* to our example from above. The *series-four list-items* are: *"To Agree"/"To Disagree."*

`0.1.4` (TO AGREE) [IS] TO EAT
`0.2.4` (TO DISAGREE) [IS] TO STARVE

[Note that for *series-four* (and afterward), you also have to insert an *"is"* between the variable *list-item* and the reoccurring *root* in order to complete each *command-line.* None of this was *Implanted* in *human-language.* Inserting *"is"* helps the *item-line* make more sense in order to properly *contact* and *process-out* its *meaning.*]

[Although it does not appear in the *Implant,* it is possible that we put some *charge* on the above examples during instruction. Your first *processing-action* might be to make sure *they* don't *register* on a *GSR-Meter;* or if you feel anything related to them, *defragment* it by the same methods you have *processed-out* other *items.*]

This *Implant* first occurs on the *Backtrack* many *Universes* ago, when *Implanting* methods were far more *"energetic"* or *"telepathic"*—relative to the heavier *"electronic" incidents* that take place in *this*

Physical Universe. But, early on, *Implants* took a lot of *energy,* and required a lot of *"time,"* just to get an *Alpha-Spirit* to "budge" even a little bit on their *considerations.*

Of course, *this Implant* is incredibly lengthy; but at the time it first occurs, *Alpha-Spirits* had a far different appreciation of relative *"time-spans"* than we do today. While an individual *Implanting-Incident* was seldom very effective early on, the *Implanting* repeatedly continued on the *Backtrack.* It cumulatively "built-up" upon its own foundations; and other *Platforms* often added to it, by restimulating it, and reducing an individual's *Awareness* enough to accept installation of some new *Implant.*

Data for any original *incident* is limited. The *Implanting-gimmick* used for this is: projecting *energy-waves* at the *Alpha-Spirit* from opposing sides. The early *series-runs* come from *left* and right. Later *series* have them come from *front* and *back,* then eventually *above* and *below*. The "positive" *command-item* of each *pair* comes from a "*golden sphere*"; the "negative" one comes from a "*silver sphere.*" There is also a "*dark explosion*" that sends out "*sheets of black energy.*"

Only a "short-form" formula is given for what would otherwise require *35,000 command-lines* to write out fully. [A *Seeker* is *not expected* to have to *run every series* to *disperse* the *Implant* anyways.] However, this is still an experimental *Platform*. We cannot yet instruct with certainty on whether or not a *Seeker* should take *charge* off of the reoccurring "*ending roots*" of the *Platform* prior to *processing-out* the *Implant*.

–It *is,* however, best practices to lightly "*scan*" for, and handle, any "*misunderstood words*" before *running* the *Implant*.

–It *is* also best practices to *discharge* the variable "*list-item*" to be inserted at the top of each *series-run,* as your *first command-line*. For example: *"I Want"* and *"I Don't Want,"* and then both of them simultaneously, or as a single line—*"I Want"/ "I Don't Want."* The *variable item-list* is included in this manual after the *Platform formula* (below).

–In that same style, although it is not indicated here: it is common to *process-out* each of the *command-lines* in a pair, on their own, and then to *run* a *third command-line* combining them and making sure that no "residual" *registers* on a *GSR-Meter.* A *Seeker* will have noticed this *combined-line* from their previous study/ use of some *Implant-Platforms.*

While combining pair-*lines* for a third *is* a common practice, given the current experimental state of this material, we cannot at this time say with certainty if it should be observed here. Further work is still required to perfectly refine *Wizard Level-3,* in addition to completing research and developing additional *Wizard-Levels* (as described in *AT#8*).

SPIRITUAL-DISABILITY PLATFORM

1.1.X ___ TO ESCAPE
1.2.X ___ TO BE CAPTURED

2.1.X ___ TO START
2.2.X ___ TO STOP

3.1.X ___ TO GO FORWARD
3.2.X ___ TO GO BACK

4.1.X ___ TO BE AWAKE
4.2.X ___ TO BE ASLEEP

5.1.X ___ TO BE COMPETENT
5.2.X ___ TO BE INCOMPETENT

6.1.X ___ TO REMEMBER
6.2.X ___ TO FORGET

7.1.X ___ TO BE LIGHT
7.2.X ___ TO BE HEAVY

8.1.X ___ TO BE TREATED HONESTLY
8.2.X ___ TO BE FOOLED

9.1.X ___ TO BE ALLOWED TO REMAIN
9.2.X ___ TO BE DRIVEN AWAY

10.1.X ___ TO BE AWARE
10.2.X ___ TO GO UNCONSCIOUS

11.1.X ___ TO BE ABLE TO STOP
11.2.X ___ TO BE MADE TO CONTINUE

12.1.X ___ TO BE FINISHED WITH THIS IMPLANT
12.2.X ___ TO BEGIN THIS IMPLANT

13.1.X ___ TO BE UNSPINNING
13.2.X ___ TO BE DIZZY

14.1.X ___ TO BE ABLE TO FIND OUT
14.2.X ___ TO BE UNABLE TO FIND OUT

15.1.X ___ TO BE PERCEPTIVE
15.2.X ___ TO BE BLIND

16.1.X ___ TO BE REPLENISHED
16.2.X ___ TO BE DRAINED

17.1.X ___ TO BE ENERGETIC
17.2.X ___ TO BE TIRED

18.1.X ___ TO BE LIVELY

18.2.X ___ TO BE IN A STUPOR

19.1.X ___ TO WAKE UP
19.2.X ___ TO BE KNOCKED OUT

20.1.X ___ TO BE BLESSED
20.2.X ___ TO BE CURSED

21.1.X ___ TO KEEP TRACK OF THINGS
21.2.X ___ TO LOSE TRACK OF THINGS

22.1.X ___ TO FOCUS ATTENTION
22.2.X ___ TO BE DISTRACTED

23.1.X ___ TO GET MOVING
23.2.X ___ TO GET STUCK

24.1.X ___ TO BE FORGIVEN
24.2.X ___ TO BE BLAMED

25.1.X ___ TO DO WHAT I'M DOING
25.2.X ___ TO DO SOMETHING ELSE

26.1.X ___ TO DO WELL
26.2.X ___ TO DO POORLY

27.1.X ___ TO FEEL PLEASURE
27.2.X ___ TO FEEL PAIN

28.1.X ___ TO BE CONFORTED

28.2.X ___ TO BE TORTURED

29.1.X ___ TO BE HEALTHY
29.2.X ___ TO BE SICK

30.1.X ___ TO BE CREATED
30.2.X ___ TO BE DESTROYED

31.1.X ___ TO BE UNTOUCHED
31.2.X ___ TO BE IMPACTED

32.1.X ___ TO BE ORIENTED
32.2.X ___ TO BE DISORIENTED

33.1.X ___ TO BE CAPABLE OF THINKING
33.2.X ___ TO BE INCAPABLE OF THINKING

34.1.X ___ TO DO ENOUGH
34.2.X ___ TO DO TOO LITTLE

35.1.X ___ TO FIND THINGS
35.2.X ___ TO LOSE THINGS

36.1.X ___ TO BE HARD TO FOOL
36.2.X ___ TO BE EASY TO FOOL

37.1.X ___ TO BE REWARDED
37.2.X ___ TO BE PUNISHED

38.1.X ___ TO BE PLEASED

38.2.X ___ TO BE DISAPPOINTED

39.1.X ___ TO BE FREE

39.2.X ___ TO BE TRAPPED

40.1.X ___ TO BE REFRESHED

40.2.X ___ TO BE WORN DOWN

41.1.X ___ TO BE PATIENT

41.2.X ___ TO BE IMPATIENT

42.1.X ___ TO ACCEPT THINGS

42.2.X ___ TO BE ANXIOUS ABOUT THINGS

43.1.X ___ TO HAVE CONFIDENCE

43.2.X ___ TO HAVE DOUBTS

44.1.X ___ TO BE TROUBLE-FREE

44.2.X ___ TO HAVE TROUBLE

45.1.X ___ TO BE MANIFESTED (*made*)

45.2.X ___ TO BE UNMANIFESTED (*unmade*)

46.1.X ___ TO HAVE AN IDENTITY

46.2.X ___ TO BE NOBODY

47.1.X ___ TO BE AN INDIVIDUAL

47.2.X ___ TO BE PART OF A COMPOSITE

48.1.X ___ TO HAVE FREE WILL
48.2.X ___ TO BE CONTROLLED

49.1.X ___ TO BE JUSTIFIED
49.2.X ___ TO BE UNJUSTIFIED

50.1.X ___ TO BE PROPER
50.2.X ___ TO BE SCANDALOUS

51.1.X ___ TO HAVE PRIDE
51.2.X ___ TO BE ASHAMED

52.1.X ___ TO BE EARLY
52.2.X ___ TO BE LATE

53.1.X ___ TO BE RELAXED
53.2.X ___ TO BE NERVOUS

54.1.X ___ TO PAY ATTENTION
54.2.X ___ TO IGNORE THINGS

55.1.X ___ TO BE CERTAIN
55.2.X ___ TO BE CONFUSED

56.1.X ___ TO HAVE A FUTURE
56.2.X ___ TO BE DOOMED

57.1.X ___ TO HAVE PLEASANT SENSATIONS
57.2.X ___ TO HAVE DISTURBING SENSATIONS

58.1.X ___ TO BE AGREED WITH
58.2.X ___ TO HAVE ARGUMENTS

59.1.X ___ TO HAVE FEELING
59.2.X ___ TO FEEL NUMB

60.1.X ___ TO HOLD TOGETHER
60.2.X ___ TO FALL APART

61.1.X ___ TO BE ETHICAL
61.2.X ___ TO BE IMMORAL

62.1.X ___ TO BE NICE
62.2.X ___ TO BE NASTY

63.1.X ___ TO BE GIVEN THINGS
63.2.X ___ TO BE DEPRIVED OF THINGS

64.1.X ___ TO FEEL COMFORTABLE
64.2.X ___ TO FEEL STRAINED

65.1.X ___ TO BE WHOLESOME
65.2.X ___ TO BE INFECTED

66.1.X ___ TO BE ALLOWED TO CONTINUE
66.2.X ___ TO BE INTERFERED WITH

67.1.X ___ TO BE SPECIAL
67.2.X ___ TO BE MUNDANE

68.1.X ___ TO CONCENTRATE
68.2.X ___ TO BE DISPERSED

69.1.X ___ TO BE WILLING
69.2.X ___ TO BE UNWILLING

70.1.X ___ TO BE SUPERIOR
70.2.X ___ TO BE INFERIOR

71.1.X ___ TO BE CLEAN
71.2.X ___ TO BE INFESTED

72.1.X ___ TO BE SPACIOUS
72.2.X ___ TO BE SOLID

73.1.X ___ TO BE COOL
73.2.X ___ TO BURN

74.1.X ___ TO BE WARM
74.2.X ___ TO FREEZE

75.1.X ___ TO FEEL SAFE
75.2.X ___ TO BE AFRAID

76.1.X ___ TO PROTECT MYSELF
76.2.X ___ TO RUIN MYSELF

77.1.X ___ TO BE NOBLE
77.2.X ___ TO BE DEGRADED

78.1.X ___ TO FEEL COMPLACENT
78.2.X ___ TO FEEL WORRIED

79.1.X ___ TO AVOID GRIEF
79.2.X ___ TO BE GRIEF-STRICKEN

80.1.X ___ TO FEEL RELIEF
80.2.X ___ TO FEEL PRESSURE

81.1.X ___ TO BE SETTLED
81.2.X ___ TO BE HYPER-ACTIVE

82.1.X ___ TO BE RESTED
82.2.X ___ TO BE UNABLE TO REST

83.1.X ___ TO BE ACCURATE
83.2.X ___ TO MAKE MISTAKES

84.1.X ___ TO BE KNOWING
84.2.X ___ TO BE UNKNOWING

85.1.X ___ TO SEE THINGS CLEARLY
85.2.X ___ TO HAVE DISTORTED PERCEPTIONS

86.1.X ___ TO BE LUCKY
86.2.X ___ TO BE UNLUCKY

87.1.X ___ TO AVOID ACCIDENTS
87.2.X ___ TO HAVE ACCIDENTS

88.1.X ___ TO BE FAVORED
88.2.X ___ TO BE PICKED ON

89.1.X ___ TO BE SMART

89.2.X ___ TO BE DUMB

90.1.X ___ TO HAVE PURPOSE
90.2.X ___ TO BE PURPOSELESS

91.1.X ___ TO BE A PART OF THINGS
91.2.X ___ TO BE DETACHED

92.1.X ___ TO HAVE INTERESTS
92.2.X ___ TO BE UNINTERESTED

93.1.X ___ TO DO THE RIGHT AMOUNT
93.2.X ___ TO DO TOO MUCH

94.1.X ___ TO BE GUIDED
94.2.X ___ TO BE MISLED

95.1.X ___ TO BE BLOCKED
95.2.X ___ TO BE UNBLOCKED

96.1.X ___ TO HAVE OPEN PERCEPTIONS
96.2.X ___ TO BE COVERED IN BLACKNESS

97.1.X ___ TO BE RATIONAL
97.2.X ___ TO BE IRRATIONAL

98.1.X ___ TO HAVE CORRECT RECOLLECTIONS
98.2.X ___ TO MISREMEMBER

99.1.X ___ TO BE UNBOTHERED
99.2.X ___ TO BE RESTIMULATED

100.1.X ___ TO DO WHAT IS NEEDED
100.2.X ___ TO OMIT THINGS

101.1.X ___ TO BE CAREFUL
101.2.X ___ TO BE CARELESS

102.1.X ___ TO BE ABLE
102.2.X ___ TO BE INCAPABLE

103.1.X ___ TO REACH
103.2.X ___ TO WITHDRAW

104.1.X ___ TO KNOW WHO I AM
104.2.X ___ TO BECOME CONFUSED ABOUT IDENTITY

105.1.X ___ TO TAKE CARE OF MYSELF
105.2.X ___ TO BE HELPLESS

106.1.X ___ TO BE INDUSTRIOUS
106.2.X ___ TO BE LAZY

107.1.X ___ TO BE INCLUDED IN THINGS
107.2.X ___ TO MISS OUT ON THINGS

108.1.X ___ TO BE VALIDATED (*praised*)

108.2.X ___ TO BE INVALIDATED

109.1.X ___ TO BE ADMIRED

109.2.X ___ TO BE ABHORRED

110.1.X ___ TO BE BEAUTIFUL

110.2.X ___ TO BE UGLY

111.1.X ___ TO BE BIG

111.2.X ___ TO BE SMALL

112.1.X ___ TO COMMUNICATE

112.2.X ___ TO BE UNABLE TO COMMUNICATE

113.1.X ___ TO BE COMMUNICATED WITH

113.2.X ___ TO BE IGNORED

114.1.X ___ TO CONSERVE THINGS

114.2.X ___ TO WASTE THINGS

115.1.X ___ TO PERCEIVE TRULY

115.2.X ___ TO BE DELUDED

116.1.X ___ TO BE LOCATED

116.2.X ___ TO BE LOST

117.1.X ___ TO THINK CLEARLY

117.2.X ___ TO HAVE MUDDLED THINKING

118.1.X ___ FOR EVERYTHING TO BE OBVIOUS
118.2.X ___ FOR EVERYTHING TO BE OBSCURE

119.1.X ___ TO BE ENCOURAGED
119.2.X ___ TO BE DISCOURAGED

120.1.X ___ TO BE ACCEPTED
120.2.X ___ TO BE SHUNNED

121.1.X ___ TO BE SUPPORTED
121.2.X ___ TO BE PERSECUTED

122.1.X ___ TO ESTIMATE CORRECTLY
122.2.X ___ TO MIS-ESTIMATE

123.1.X ___ TO BE COMPLETE
123.2.X ___ TO BE INCOMPLETE

124.1.X ___ TO BE ENTHUSIASTIC
124.2.X ___ TO BE DESPONDENT

125.1.X ___ TO GET THINGS RIGHT
125.2.X ___ TO GET THINGS MIXED UP

126.1.X ___ TO GET THINGS CORRECT
126.2.X ___ TO MISS THINGS

127.1.X ___ TO HAVE THINGS IN SEQUENCE

127.2.X ___ TO HAVE THINGS OUT-OF-SEQUENCE

128.1.X ___ TO IDENTIFY THINGS CORRECTLY

128.2.X ___ TO CONFUSE ONE THING WITH ANOTHER

129.1.X ___ TO DIFFERENTIATE THINGS

129.2.X ___ TO THINK THAT EVERYTHING IS THE SAME

130.1.X ___ TO BE ABLE TO KEEP THINGS TOGETHER

130.2.X ___ TO HAVE EVERYTHING FALL APART

131.1.X ___ TO BE TREATED RIGHTLY

131.2.X ___ TO BE TREATED WRONGLY

132.1.X ___ TO BE LOGICAL

132.2.X ___ TO BE ILLOGICAL

133.1.X ___ TO BE IMAGINATIVE

133.2.X ___ TO BE DULL

134.1.X ___ TO FEEL PLEASANT
134.2.X ___ TO FEEL HORRIBLE

135.1.X ___ TO BE ACCEPTING OF THINGS
135.2.X ___ TO BE REVOLTED BY THINGS

136.1.X ___ TO BE RESPONSIBLE
136.2.X ___ TO BE IRRESPONSIBLE

137.1.X ___ TO SEE REALITY
137.2.X ___ TO SEE DELUSIONS

138.1.X ___ TO BE COMPLACENT
138.2.X ___ TO BE DESPERATE

139.1.X ___ TO BE FAST
139.2.X ___ TO BE SLOW

140.1.X ___ TO BE REASONABLE
140.2.X ___ TO BE FANATICAL

141.1.X ___ TO BE RIGHT
141.2.X ___ TO BE WRONG

142.1.X ___ TO BE RICH
142.2.X ___ TO BE POOR

143.1.X ___ TO BE DECISIVE
143.2.X ___ TO BE UNABLE TO MAKE UP MY MIND

144.1.X ___ TO BE WHOLE
144.2.X ___ TO BE DIVIDED AGAINST MYSELF
145.1.X ___ TO BE CONTENTED
145.2.X ___ TO BE BOTHERED
146.1.X ___ TO BE STRONG
146.2.X ___ TO BE WEAK
147.1.X ___ TO BE ENDURING
147.2.X ___ TO BE TRANSIENT
148.1.X ___ TO BE CALM
148.2.X ___ TO BE UPSET
149.1.X ___ TO BE CAREFREE
149.2.X ___ TO BE WEIGHED DOWN
150.1.X ___ TO BE EFFECTIVE
150.2.X ___ TO BE INEFFECTIVE
151.1.X ___ TO PUT THINGS IN THE RIGHT PLACE
151.2.X ___ TO PUT THINGS IN THE WRONG PLACE
152.1.X ___ TO KNOW WHERE THINGS BELONG
152.2.X ___ TO NOT KNOW WHERE THINGS BELONG

153.1.X ___ TO KNOW WHERE THINGS ARE

153.2.X ___ TO NOT KNOW WHERE THINGS ARE

154.1.X ___ TO PUT THINGS THE RIGHT WAY AROUND

154.2.X ___ TO PUT THINGS BACKWARDS

155.1.X ___ TO BE HAPPY

155.2.X ___ TO BE SAD

156.1.X ___ TO HAVE THE WILL TO LIVE

156.2.X ___ TO BE UNWILLING TO LIVE

157.1.X ___ TO HAVE VARIETY

157.2.X ___ TO BE BORED

158.1.X ___ TO KNOW TRUTH

158.2.X ___ TO BELIEVE IN LIES

159.1.X ___ TO BE TOLD TRUTH

159.2.X ___ TO BE GIVEN FALSE DATA

160.1.X ___ TO KNOW WHAT IS REAL

160.2.X ___ TO BE UNSURE OF WHAT IS REAL

161.1.X ___ TO KNOW WHAT IS THERE

161.2.X ___ TO IMAGINE THINGS THAT AREN'T THERE

162.1.X ___ TO BE COMPLEMENTED

162.2.X ___ TO BE CRITICIZED

163.1.X ___ TO BE LOVED

163.2.X ___ TO BE HATED

164.1.X ___ TO HAVE FRIENDS

164.2.X ___ TO HAVE ENEMIES

165.1.X ___ TO HAVE ALLIES

165.2.X ___ TO HAVE OPPONENTS

166.1.X ___ TO BE LOOSE

166.2.X ___ TO BE RESTRAINED

167.1.X ___ TO HAVE CHOICES

167.2.X ___ TO HAVE NO CHOICE

168.1.X ___ TO BE ALLOWED TO PROCEED

168.2.X ___ TO BE HEMMED IN

169.1.X ___ TO BE CAUSATIVE

169.2.X ___ TO BE AT EFFECT

170.1.X ___ TO REACH THINGS

170.2.X ___ TO BE UNABLE TO REACH THINGS

171.1.X ___ TO CONTROL THINGS

171.2.X ___ TO BE UNABLE TO CONTROL THINGS

172.1.X ___ TO HAVE GAMES

172.2.X ___ TO HAVE NO GAME

173.1.X ___ TO BE SATISFIED

173.2.X ___ TO BE UNSATISFIED

174.1.X ___ TO HAVE WHAT YOU NEED

174.2.X ___ TO SUFFER FROM CRAVINGS

175.1.X ___ TO HAVE NO REGRETS

175.2.X ___ TO BE REGRETFUL

176.1.X ___ TO BE OPEN

176.2.X ___ TO BE CLOSED IN

177.1.X ___ TO ARRANGE THINGS CORRECTLY

177.2.X ___ TO MESS THINGS UP

178.1.X ___ TO SEE ACCEPTABLE THINGS

178.2.X ___ TO BE DAZZLED

179.1.X ___ TO RECEIVE SYMPATHY

179.2.X ___ TO GET NO SYMPATHY

180.1.X ___ TO GET AWAY WITH THINGS
180.2.X ___ TO BE ACCUSED
181.1.X ___ TO BE AQUITTED
181.2.X ___ TO BE CONDEMNED
182.1.X ___ TO BE LET GO
182.2.X ___ TO BE HUNTED
183.1.X ___ TO ESCAPE THE CONSEQUENCES
183.2.X ___ TO SUFFER THE CONSEQUENCES
184.1.X ___ TO AVOID BEING IMPLANTED
184.2.X ___ TO WANT TO BE IMPLANTED
185.1.X ___ TO PLEASE PEOPLE
185.2.X ___ TO UPSET PEOPLE
186.1.X ___ TO OBEY THE RULES
186.2.X ___ TO BREAK THE RULES
187.1.X ___ TO BE GOOD
187.2.X ___ TO BE EVIL
188.1.X ___ TO HELP OTHERS
188.2.X ___ TO HARM OTHERS

189.1.X ___ TO REASSURE PEOPLE

189.2.X ___ TO SHOCK PEOPLE

190.1.X ___ TO MAKE OTHERS FEEL SAFE

190.2.X ___ TO TERRORIZE OTHERS

191.1.X ___ TO HAVE NORMAL DESIRES

191.2.X ___ TO BE OBSESSED

192.1.X ___ TO BE SANE

192.2.X ___ TO BE INSANE

193.1.X ___ TO TAKE ENOUGH TIME

193.2.X ___ TO TAKE TOO LONG

194.1.X ___ TO BE INDEPENDENT

194.2.X ___ TO BE DEPENDENT

195.1.X ___ TO BE SATISFIED

195.2.X ___ TO HAVE LONGINGS

196.1.X ___ TO KNOW WHAT'S GOING ON

196.2.X ___ TO BE PUZZLED BY EVENTS

197.1.X ___ TO KNOW WHAT'S GOING TO HAPPEN

197.2.X ___ TO BE TAKEN BY SURPRISE

198.1.X ___ TO KNOW THE CONSEQUENCES

198.2.X ___ TO BE CAUGHT UNAWARE

199.1.X ___ TO BE ABLE TO ADAPT

199.2.X ___ TO BE UNABLE TO CHANGE

200.1.X ___ TO BE FLEXIBLE

200.2.X ___ TO BE RIGID

201.1.X ___ TO BE ON TIME

201.2.X ___ TO BE TOO LATE

202.1.X ___ TO BE PARTICIPATING

202.2.X ___ TO BE ALONE

203.1.X ___ TO LIKE WHAT IS GOING ON

203.2.X ___ TO DISLIKE EVERYTHING

204.1.X ___ TO BE ABLE TO PROTEST

204.2.X ___ TO HAVE TO PUT UP WITH EVERYTHING

205.1.X ___ TO BE ABLE TO CHANGE CONDITIONS

205.2.X ___ TO BE STUCK WITH THINGS AS THEY ARE

206.1.X ___ TO BE STABLE

206.2.X ___ TO BE PUSHED AROUND

207.1.X ___ TO BE ABLE TO DECIDE NOT TO DO SOMETHING

207.2.X ___ TO BE FORCED TO DO THINGS

208.1.X ___ TO BE AT THE RIGHT DISTANCE

208.2.X ___ TO BE TOO CLOSE

209.1.X ___ TO HAVE HOPE

209.2.X ___ TO BE HOPELESS

210.1.X ___ TO UNDERSTAND THINGS

210.2.X ___ TO MISUNDERSTAND THINGS

211.1.X ___ TO RECEIVE HELP

211.2.X ___ TO GET NO HELP

212.1.X ___ TO BE FAIR

212.2.X ___ TO BE UNFAIR

213.1.X ___ TO BE SHARING

213.2.X ___ TO BE SELFISH

214.1.X ___ TO HAVE THE RIGHT AMOUNT

214.2.X ___ TO HAVE TOO MUCH

215.1.X ___ TO FEEL FULL

215.2.X ___ TO FEEL EMPTY

216.1.X ___ TO BE AT THE RIGHT TIME

216.2.X ___ TO BE EARLY

217.1.X ___ TO BE IN THE RIGHT SPACE

217.2.X ___ TO BE IN THE WRONG SPACE (*place*)

218.1.X ___ TO BE KIND

218.2.X ___ TO BE CRUEL

219.1.X ___ TO BE HUMAN(E)

219.2.X ___ TO BE A MONSTER

220.1.X ___ TO BE WHERE YOU SHOULD BE

220.2.X ___ TO BE TOO FAR AWAY

221.1.X ___ TO BE SUCCESSFUL

221.2.X ___ TO BE A FAILURE

222.1.X ___ TO WIN

222.2.X ___ TO LOSE

223.1.X ___ TO FEEL RELIEVED

223.2.X ___ TO FEEL CRUSHED

224.1.X ___ TO BE DEFENDED

224.2.X ___ TO BE ATTACKED

225.1.X ___ TO BE TOUGH
225.2.X ___ TO BE OVERWHELMED

226.1.X ___ TO BE DETERMINED
226.2.X ___ TO GIVE UP

227.1.X ___ TO BE A GOOD CITIZEN
227.2.X ___ TO BE A CRIMINAL

228.1.X ___ TO BE A MEMBER OF SOCIETY
228.2.X ___ TO BE AN OUTCAST

229.1.X ___ TO SUPPORT SOCIETY
229.2.X ___ TO OVERTHROW SOCIETY

230.1.X ___ TO ADVANCE
230.2.X ___ TO BE HELD BACK

231.1.X ___ TO HAVE NICE THINGS
231.2.X ___ TO HAVE NOTHING

232.1.X ___ TO HAVE ENOUGH SPACE
232.2.X ___ TO HAVE TOO LITTLE SPACE

233.1.X ___ TO BE ALLOWED TO REMAIN
233.2.X ___ TO BE KICKED-OUT OF SPACES

234.1.X ___ TO BE WISE

234.2.X ___ TO BE FOOLISH

235.1.X ___ TO DO THINGS AT THE RIGHT TIME

235.2.X ___ TO DO THINGS AT THE WRONG TIME

236.1.X ___ TO HAVE ENOUGH TIME

236.2.X ___ TO RUN OUT OF TIME

237.1.X ___ TO RISE

237.2.X ___ TO FALL

238.1.X ___ TO GROW

238.2.X ___ TO SHRINK

239.1.X ___ TO GET BETTER

239.2.X ___ TO GET WORSE

240.1.X ___ TO BECOME MORE SUBSTANTIAL

240.2.X ___ TO GET THINNER

241.1.X ___ TO KNOW WHAT TIME IT IS

241.2.X ___ TO NOT-KNOW WHAT TIME IT IS

242.1.X ___ TO KNOW WHAT SPACE I'M IN

242.2.X ___ TO NOT-KNOW WHAT SPACE I'M IN

243.1.X ___ TO ESTIMATE TIME CORRECTLY

243.2.X ___ TO MIS-ESTIMATE TIME

244.1.X ___ TO ESTIMATE DISTANCE CORRECTLY

244.2.X ___ TO MIS-ESTIMATE DISTANCE

245.1.X ___ TO HAVE FAITH

245.2.X ___ TO HAVE DISBELIEF

246.1.X ___ TO BE ENLIGHTENED

246.2.X ___ TO BE MYSTIFIED

247.1.X ___ TO SPOT THE SOURCE OF THINGS

247.2.X ___ TO SPOT THE WRONG SOURCE

248.1.X ___ TO PLEASE 'GOD'

248.2.X ___ TO DISPLEASE 'GOD'

249.1.X ___ TO OBEY 'GOD'

249.2.X ___ TO DEFY 'GOD'

250.1.X ___ TO BE SAVED

250.2.X ___ TO BE DAMNED

251.1.X ___ TO BE IN HEAVEN
251.2.X ___ TO BE IN HELL

252.1.X ___ TO BE ALIVE
252.2.X ___ TO BE DEAD

253.1.X ___ TO BE IN PARADISE FOREVER
253.2.X ___ TO BURN IN HELL FOREVER

254.1.X ___ TO CREATE
254.2.X ___ TO DESTROY

255.1.X ___ TO HAVE REALITY
255.2.X ___ TO FEEL UNREAL

256.1.X ___ TO HAVE THE RIGHT TIME
256.2.X ___ TO HAVE THE WRONG TIME

257.1.X ___ TO HAVE THE RIGHT SPACE
257.2.X ___ TO HAVE THE WRONG SPACE

258.1.X ___ TO HAVE THE RIGHT ENERGY
258.2.X ___ TO HAVE THE WRONG ENERGY

259.1.X ___ TO HAVE THE RIGHT MASS

259.2.X ___ TO HAVE THE WRONG MASS

260.1.X ___ TO BE REAL

260.2.X ___ TO BE UNREAL

261.1.X ___ TO BE RIGHT ABOUT TIME

261.2.X ___ TO BE WRONG ABOUT TIME

262.1.X ___ TO BE RIGHT ABOUT SPACE

262.2.X ___ TO BE WRONG ABOUT SPACE

263.1.X ___ TO BE RIGHT ABOUT ENERGY

263.2.X ___ TO BE WRONG ABOUT ENERGY

264.1.X ___ TO BE RIGHT ABOUT MASS

264.2.X ___ TO BE WRONG ABOUT MASS

265.1.X ___ TO BE RIGHT ABOUT EXISTENCE

265.2.X ___ TO BE WRONG ABOUT EXISTENCE

266.1.X ___ TO HAVE MASS
266.2.X ___ TO HAVE NO MASS

267.1.X ___ TO HAVE ENERGY
267.2.X ___ TO HAVE NO ENERGY

268.1.X ___ TO HAVE SPACE
268.2.X ___ TO HAVE NO SPACE

269.1.X ___ TO HAVE TIME
269.2.X ___ TO HAVE NO TIME

270.1.X ___ TO HAVE A UNIVERSE
270.2.X ___ TO HAVE NO UNIVERSE

271.1.X ___ TO HAVE EXISTENCE
271.2.X ___ TO HAVE NO EXISTENCE

[*Research Notes*: There may or may not be missing *command-lines* around *pair-61* and *pair-62,* regarding dichotomies of *"Immortal"/"Age"* and *"Young"/"Old"*; but this is not certain. This *Platform* has proven quite effective as-is, though more experimental testing is still required for its standardization.]

VARIABLE LIST-ITEMS MASTER-LIST

Each of the following lines is an entire *series-run* of the previous *Implant-pattern.* By combining the two, you have the content for the entire *Platform.* Refer to the earlier instructions for details on inserting the variable *list-items* from this *master-list.* For example: the *first command-lines* for the *first series-run* are:

1.1.1 I WANT TO ESCAPE
1.2.1 I DON'T WANT TO BE CAPTURED

The same *"I Want"/"I Don't Want" item* is then applied to each of the *271* dichotomy-pairs to complete the *first series-run.* Then proceed to the top of the *Implant-pattern* and insert the next set of *list-items,* and so on.

This *master-list* is effective as given. However, our A.T. researchers would *usually* end up *defragging* the whole *Platform* after *running* a few dozen *series,* leaving the remainder to be plotted out mainly by *assessment* and *research-actions* (see *AT#8*). Further into the *master-list* (beyond *item-31*), it is possible that some of the *items* are incorrect, improperly ordered, or altogether missing. More experimental testing is needed for standardization.

[Note that on specifically the *third series-run*, when inserting the negative *"I must not"* on the second item of each pair in the *pattern*, you will have to remove the word *"to"* from the *pattern-line*.]

BEINGNESS CONDITIONS (SERIES-RUNS)

1. I want / I don't want
2. I need / I can't bear
3. I have / I must not

REALITY PERCEPTION (SERIES-RUNS)

4. To agree / To disagree
5. To obey / To disobey
6. To do nothing with the mind / To do anything with the mind
7. To be unaware of this / To be aware of this

8. To not figure this out / To figure this out
9. To resist change / To try to change
10. To be in a body / To be outside a body
11. To interiorize (*go inside*) / To exteriorize (*eject*)
12. To keep this implant / To undo this implant
13. To generalize / To identify
14. To associate / To disassociate
15. To not look / To look
16. To not scan / To scan
17. To synchronize with reality / To desynchronize from reality
18. To fixate on physical reality / To shift n reality
19. To limit myself to three dimensions / To extend beyond three dimensions
20. To be aware of only three dimensions / To be aware of more than three dimensions

FRAGMENT / DEFRAGMENT (SERIES)

21. To not heal / To heal

22. To not cure / To cure
23. To entrap others / To release others
24. To enturbulate others / To unenturbulate others
25. To aberrate / To deaberrate
26. To block others / To unblock others
27. To inhibit others / To uninhibit others
28. To not process-out / To process-out
29. To not clear / To clear
(*or*) To not defragment / To defragment
30. To not restore / To restore

REALITY-STRUCTURING (SERIES-RUNS)

31. To create physical reality / To not create physical reality
32. To not duplicate / To duplicate
33. To not replicate / To replicate
34. To cross-copy / To not cross-copy
35. To not program thoughts / To program thoughts
36. To respond to programmed thoughts / To ignore programmed thoughts
37. To be unaware of machinery / To be aware of machinery

38. To not create machinery / To create machinery
39. To ignore mental machinery / To control mental machinery
40. To be the effect of mental machinery / To be unaffected by mental machinery
41. To obey universe machinery / To disobey universe machinery
42. To hide universe machinery / To notice universe machinery

LOCATED-BEINGNESS (SERIES-RUNS)

43. To be in one place / To be in many places
44. To not see the structure of things / To see the structure of things
45. To not see through things / To see through things
46. To not look within things / To look within things
47. To not-know / To know
48. To not see remotely / To see remotely
49. To not locate / To locate
50. To not pervade / To pervade

51. To not permeate / To permeate
52. To not dimensionalize / To dimensionalize
53. To see it-as-not / To see as-it-is

TIME-STRUCTURING (SERIES-RUNS)

54. To agree with the time-stream / To leave the time-stream
55. To be wrong about time / To spot the correct time
56. To have a time-track / To have no time-track
57. To take time / To bypass time
58. To be the effect of time / To ignore time
59. To maintain the present / To change the past

ENTITY-FRAGMENTS (SERIES-RUNS)

60. To be the effect of entities / To not be the effect of entities
61. To hold on to entities / To let go of entities
62. To obey entities / To disobey entities
63. To block entities from view / To see entities

64. To be infested / To be clean
65. To infest others / To clean others
66. To be divided against myself / To be whole
67. To fragment / To integrate

SOLIDIFICATION (SERIES-RUNS)

68. To not orient anchor-points / To orient anchor-points
69. To not determinate objects / To determinate objects
70. To leave the structure of things alone / To manipulate (*change*) the structure of things
71. To not make things materialize / To make things materialize
72. To not dematerialize / To dematerialize
73. To make solids impenetrable / To make solids penetrable
74. To not infinitize / To infinitize
75. To not actualize / To actualize
76. To perpetuate reality / To violate reality
77. To leave random / To unrandomize

78. To not read minds / To read minds
79. To not take over other's minds / To take over other's minds
80. To not alter other's minds / To alter other's minds
81. To not implode other's pictures / To implode other's pictures
82. To not swap thoughts / To swap thoughts
83. To not project thoughts / To project thoughts
84. To not endow life / To endow life
85. To not manipulate life-force / To manipulate life-force
86. To not drain life-force / To drain life-force

ABILITY-SUPPRESSION (SERIES-RUNS)

87. To not intend / To intend
88. To not postulate / To postulate
89. To not levitate / To levitate
90. To not teleport / To teleport
91. To not manipulate energy / To manipulate energy
92. To not create energy / To create energy

93. To propagate flows / To dampen flows
94. To not glare (*stare down*) / To glare (*stare down*)
95. To not beam / To beam
96. To not blanket / To blanket
97. To not zap / To zap
98. To not nip / To nip
99. To not manifest / To manifest
100. To not spaceate / To spaceate
101. To not energize / To energize
102. To not historicize / To historicize (?)
103. To maintain a single viewpoint / To maintain multiple viewpoints
104. To need mass / To do without mass
105. To need energy / To do without energy
106. To need time / To do without time
107. To need space / To do without space (?)
108. To fill space / To have space (?)
109. To be located / To not be located
110. To gain mass / To lose mass
111. To be affected by energy / To ignore energy

112. To deteriorate / To improve
113. To follow the laws of energy / To violate the laws of energy
114. To follow the laws of space / To violate the laws of space
115. To follow the laws of time / To violate the laws of time
116. To follow the laws of matter / To violate the laws of matter
117. To not predict / To predict
118. To not predetermine / To predetermine
119. To not find out / To find out
120. To perceive as a body / To perceive as a spirit
121. To operate as a body / To operate as a spirit
122. To be a body / To be a spirit
123. To be "human" / To be god-like
124. To be in this universe / To leave this universe

Your next Advanced Training manual is:
"Advancing Systemology"

BASIC SYSTEMOLOGY GLOSSARY

actualization : to make actual, not just potential; to bring into full solid Reality; to realize fully in *Awareness* as a "thing."

agreement (reality) : unanimity of opinion of what is "thought" to be known; an accepted arrangement of how things are; things we consider as "real" or as an "is" of "reality"; a consensus of what is real as made by standard-issue (common) participants; what an individual contributes to or accepts as "real"; in *Systemology*, a synonym for "*reality*."

alpha : the first, primary, basic, superior or beginning of some form; in *Systemology*, referring to the state of existence operating on spiritual archetypes and postulates, will and intention "exterior" to the low-level condensation and solidarity of energy and matter as the 'physical universe' (*beta*).

alpha-spirit : a "spiritual" *Life*-form; the "true" *Self* or I-AM; the *individual*; the spiritual (*alpha*) *Self* that is animating the (*beta*) physical body or "*genetic vehicle*" using a continuous *Lifeline* of spiritual ("*ZU*") energy; an individual spiritual (*alpha*) entity possessing no physical mass or measurable waveform (motion) in the Physical Universe as itself, so it animates the (*beta*) physical body or "*genetic vehicle*" as a catalyst to experience *Self*-determined causality in effect within the *Physical Universe*; a singular unit or point of *Spiritual Awareness* that is *Aware* that it is *Aware.*

alpha thought : the highest spiritual *Self-determination* over creation and existence exercised by an Alpha-Spirit; the Alpha range of pure *Creative Ability* based on direct postulates and considerations of *Beingness*; spiritual qualities comparable to "thought" but originating in Alpha-existence, independently superior to a Mind-System.

ascension : actualized *Awareness* elevated to the point of true "spiritual existence" exterior to *beta existence*. An "Ascended Master" is one who has returned to an incarnation on Earth as an inherently *Enlightened One*, demonstrable in their words and actions; they have the ability to *Self-direct* the "Mind" and "Body" as *Self* (as a "Spirit"); and to maintain consciousness as a personal identity continuum with the same *Self-directed* control and communication of Will-Intention that is exercised, actualized and developed deliberately during one's present incarnation.

associative knowledge : significance or meaning of a facet or aspect assigned to (or considered to have) a direct relationship with another facet; to connect or relate ideas or facets of existence with one another; in traditional systems logic, an equivalency of significance or meaning between facets or sets that are grouped together, such as in $(a + b) + c = a + (b + c)$; in Systemology, erroneous associative knowledge is assignment of the same value to all facets or parts considered as related (even when they are not actually so), such as in $a = a$, $b = a$, $c = a$ and so forth without distinction.

attention : active use of *Awareness* toward a specific aspect or thing; the act of "attending" with the presence of *Self*; a direction of focus or concentration of *Awareness* along a particular channel or conduit or toward a particular terminal node or communication termination point; the Self-directed concentration of personal energy as a combination of observation, thought-waves and consideration; focused application of *Self-Directed Awareness*.

awareness : the highest sense of-and-as *Self* in knowing and being as I-AM (the *Alpha-Spirit*); the extent of beingness directed as a viewpoint (POV) experienced by *Self* as *Knowingness*.

beta (awareness) : all consciousness activity ("*Awareness*") in the "Physical Universe" (KI, in *Zuism*) or else in *beta-existence*; *Awareness* within the range of the *genetic-body*, including material thoughts, emotional responses and physical motors; personal *Awareness* of physical energy and physical matter moving through physical space and experienced as "time"; the *Awareness* held by *Self* that is restricted to an organic *Lifeform* or "*genetic vehicle*" in which it experiences causality in *beta-existence*.

beta (existence) : all manifestation in the "Physical Universe" (KI, in *Zuism*); the conditions of *Awareness* for the *Alpha-spirit* (*Self*) as a physical organic *Lifeform* or "*genetic vehicle*" in which it experiences causality in the *Physical Universe*.

charge : to fill or furnish with a quality; to supply with energy; to lay a command upon; in *Systemology*—to imbue with intention; to overspread with emotion; personal energy stores and significances entwined as fragmentation in mental images, reactive-response encoding and intellectual (and/or) programmed beliefs.

channel : a specific stream, course, current, direction or route; to form or cut a groove or ridge or otherwise guide along a specific course; a direct path; an artificial aqueduct created to connect two water bodies or water or make travel possible.

circuit : a circular path or loop; a closed-path within a system that allows a flow; a pattern or action or wave movement that follows a specific route or potential path only; in *Systemology*, "*communication processing*" pertaining to a specific *flow* of energy or information along a channel; "*feedback loop.*"

communication : successful transmission of information, data, energy (&tc.) along a message line, with a reception of feedback; an energetic flow of intention to cause an effect (or duplication) at a distance; the personal energy moved or acted upon by will or else 'selective directed attention'; the 'messenger action' used to transmit and receive energy across a medium; also relay of energy, a message or signal—or even locating a personal POV (viewpoint) for the Self—along the *ZU-line*.

condense (condensation) : the transition of vapor to liquid; denoting a change in state to a more substantial or solid condition; leading to a more compact or solid form.

confront : to come around in front of; to be in the presence of; to stand in front of, or in the face of; to meet "face-to-face" or "face-up-to"; additionally, in *Systemology*, to fully tolerate or acceptably withstand an encounter with a particular manifestation without an automatic reactive response.

consideration : careful analytical reflection of all aspects; deliberation; determining the significance of a "thing" in relation to similarity or dissimilarity to other "things"; evaluation of facts and importance of certain facts; thorough examination of all aspects related to, or important for, making a decision; the analysis of consequences and estimation of significance when making decisions; also in *Systemology*, the *postulate* or *Alpha-Thought* that defines the state of *beingness* for what something "*is.*"

defragmentation : the *reparation* of wholeness; collecting all dispersed parts to reform an original whole; a process of removing "*fragmentation*" in data or knowledge to provide a clear understanding; applying techniques and processes that promote a *holistic* interconnected *alpha* state, favoring observational *Awareness* of continuity in all spiritual and physical systems; in *Systemology*, a "*Seeker*" achieving actualized "*Self-Honest Awareness*" is said to be in a basic state of *beta-defragmentation*, whereas *Alpha-defragmentation* is the rehabilitation of the *creative ability*, managing the *Spiritual Timeline* and the POV of *Self* as Alpha-Spirit (I-AM).

existence : the *state* or fact of *apparent manifestation*; the resulting combination of the Principles of Manifestation: consciousness, motion and substance; continued *survival*; that which independently exists.

exterior : outside of; on the outside; in *Systemology*, we mean specifically the POV of *Self* that is *'outside of'* the *Human Condition,* free of the physical and mental trappings of the Physical Universe; a metahuman range of consideration; see also '*Zu-Vision*'.

external : a force coming from outside; information received from outside sources; in *Systemology*, the objective *'Physical Universe'* existence, or *beta-existence*, that the Physical Body or *genetic vehicle* is essentially *anchored* to for its considerations of locational space-time as a dimension or POV.

fragmentation : breaking into parts and scattering the pieces; the *fractioning* of wholeness or the *fracture* of a holistic interconnected *alpha* state, favoring observational *Awareness* of perceived connectivity between parts; *discontinuity*; separation of a totality into parts; in *Systemology*, a person outside of *Self-Honesty* is said to be operating from a *fragmented* state.

flow : movement across (or through) a channel (or conduit); a direction of active energetic motion, typically distinguished as either an *in-flow, out-flow* or *cross-flow.*

genetic-vehicle : a physical *Life*-form; the physical (*beta*) body that is animated/controlled by the (*Alpha*) *Spirit* using a continuous *Spiritual Lifeline* (ZU); a physical (*beta*) organic receptacle and catalyst for the (*Alpha*) *Self* to operate "causes" and experience "effects" within the *Physical Universe*.

harmful-act : a counter-survival mode of behavior or action (esp. that causes harm to one of more *Spheres of Existence*)—or—an overtly aggressive (hostile and/or destructive) action against an individual or any other *Sphere of Existence*; in *Utilitarian Systemology*—a shortsighted (serves fewest/lowest *Spheres of Existence*) intentional overtly harmful action to resolve a perceived problem; a revision of the rule for standard *Utilitarianism* for Systemology to distinguish actions which provide the least benefit to the least number of *Spheres of Existence*, or else the greatest harm to the greatest number of *Spheres of Existence*; in *moral philosophy*—an action which can be experienced by few and/or which one would not be willing to experience for themselves (*theft, slander, rape, &tc*); an iniquity or iniquitous act.

hold-back : withheld communications (esp. actions) such as "*Hold-Outs*"; intentional (or automatic) withdrawal (as opposed to reach); Self-restraint (which may eventually be enforced or automated); not reaching, acting or expressing, when one should be; an ability that is now restrained (on automatic) due to inability to withhold it on Self-determinism alone.

hold-outs : in photography, the numerous snapshots/pictures withheld from the final display or professional presentation of the event; withheld communications; in Utilitarian Systemology—energetic withdrawal and communication breaks with a "*terminal*" and its *Sphere of Existence* as a result of a "*Harmful-Act*"; unspoken or undiscovered (hidden, covert) actions that an individual withholds communications of, fearing punishment or endangerment of *Self-preservation* (*First Sphere*); the act of hiding (or keeping hidden) the truth of a "*Harmful-Act*"; a refusal to communicate with a *Pilot*; also "*Hold-Back.*"

holistic : the examination of interconnected systems as encompassing something greater than the *sum* of their "parts."

Human Condition : a standard default state of Human experience that is generally accepted to be the extent of its potential identity (*beingness*) —currently treated as *Homo Sapiens Sapiens,* but which is scheduled for replacement by *Homo Novus* (the "New Human").

imagination : ability to create *mental imagery* in one's Personal Universe at will and change or alter it as desired; the ability to create, change and dissolve mental images on command or as an act of will; to create a mental image or have associated imagery displayed (or "conjured") in the mind that may or may not be treated as real (or memory recall) and may or may not accurately duplicate objective reality; to employ *creative abilities* of the Spirit that are independent of reality agreements with beta-existence.

imprint : to strongly impress, stamp, mark (or outline) onto a softer 'impressible' substance; to mark with pressure onto a surface; in *Systemology*, used to indicate permanent Reality impressions marked by frequencies, energies or interactions experienced during periods of emotional distress, pain, unconsciousness, loss, enforcement, or something antagonistic to physical (personal) survival, all of which are are stored with other reactive response-mechanisms at lower-levels of *Awareness* as opposed to the active memory database and proactive processing center of the Mind; an experiential "memory-set" that may later resurface—be triggered or stimulated artificially—as Reality, of which similar responses will be engaged automatically; holographic-like imagery "stamped" onto consciousness as composed of energetic *facets* tied to the "snap-shot" of an experience.

imprinting incident : the first or original event

instance communicated and *emotionally encoded* onto an individual's "*Spiritual Timeline*" (recorded memory from all lifetimes), which formed a permanent impression that is later used to mechanistically treat future contact on that channel; the first or original occurrence of some particular *facet* or mental image related to a certain type of *encoded response*, such as pain and discomfort, losses and victimization, and even the acts that we have taken against others along the *Spiritual Timeline* of our existence that caused them to also be *Imprinted*.

intention : directed application of Will; to intend (have "in Mind") or signify (give "significance" to) for or toward a particular purpose; in *Systemology* (from the *Standard Model*)—the spiritual activity at WILL (5.0) directed by an *Alpha Spirit* (7.0); the application of WILL as "Cause" from a higher order of Alpha Thought and consideration (6.0).

interior : inside of; on the inside; in *Systemology*, we mean specifically the POV of *Self* that is fixed to the *'internal' Human Condition,* including the *Reactive Control Center* (RCC) and Mind-System or *Master Control Center* (MCC); within *beta-existence.*

internal : a force coming from inside; information received from inside sources; in *Systemology*, the objective experience of *beta-existence* associated with the Physical Body or *genetic vehicle* and its POV regarding sensation and perception; from inside the body; in the body.

invalidate : decrease the level or degree or *agreement* as Reality.

mental image : a subjectively experienced "picture" created and imagined into being by the Alpha-Spirit (or at lower levels, one of its automated mechanisms) that includes all perceptible *facets* of totally immersive scene, which may be forms originated by an individual, or a "facsimile-copy" ("snap-shot") of something seen or encountered; a duplication of wave-forms in one's Personal Universe as a "picture" that mirror an "external" Universe experience, such as an *Imprint*.

perception : internalized processing of data received by the *senses*; to become *Aware of* via the senses.

pilot : a professional steersman responsible for healthy functional operation of a ship toward a specific destination; in *Systemology*, an intensive trained individual qualified to specially apply *Systemology Processing* to assist other *Seekers* on the *Pathway*.

point-of-view (POV) : a point to view from; an opinion or attitude as expressed from a specific identity-phase; a specific standpoint or vantage-point; a definitive manner of consideration specific to an individual phase or identity; a place or position affording a specific view or vantage; circumstances and programming of an individual that is conducive to a particular response, consideration or belief-set (paradigm); a position (consideration) or place (location) that provides a specific view or perspective (subjective) on experience (of the objective).

postulate : to put forward as truth; to suggest or assume an existence *to be*; to state or affirm the existence of particular conditions; to provide a basis of reasoning and belief; a basic theory accepted as fact; in *Systemology*, Alpha-Thought —the top-most decisions or considerations made by the Alpha-Spirit regarding the "*isness*" (what things "are") about energy-matter and space-time.

presence : a quality of some thing (*energy/matter*) being "present" in space-time; personal orientation of *Self* as an *Awareness* (*POV*) located in present space-time (environment) and communicating with extant energy-matter.

processing command line (PCL) : a directed input; a specific command using highly selective language for *Systemology Processing*; a predetermined directive statement (cause) intended to focus concentrated attention (effect).

processing, systematic : the inner-workings or "through-put" result of systems; in *Systemology*, a method of applied spiritual technology used toward personal Self-Actualization; methods of selective directed attention, communicated language and associative imagery that increases personal control of the human condition.

realization : the clear perception of an understanding; a consideration or understanding on what is "actual"; to make "real" or give "reality" to so as to grant a property of "beingness" or "being as it is"; the state or instance of coming to an *Awareness*; in *Systemology*, "gnosis" or true knowledge achieved during *systematic processing*; achievement of a new (or higher) cognition, true knowledge or perception of Self; a consideration of reality or assignment of meaning.

responsibility : the *ability* to *respond*; the extent of mobilizing *power* and *understanding* an individual maintains as *Awareness* to enact *change*; the proactive ability to *Self-direct* and make decisions independent of an outside authority.

Seeker : an individual on the *Pathway to Self-Honesty*; a practitioner of *Mardukite Systemology* or *Systemology Processing*, that is working toward *Spiritual Ascension*.

Self-actualization : bringing the full potential of the Human spirit into Reality; expressing full capabilities and creativeness of the *Alpha-Spirit*.

Self-determinism : the freedom to act, clear of external control or influence; the personal control of Will to direct intention.

Self-honesty : the basic or original *alpha* state of *being* and *knowing*; clear and present total *Awareness* of-and-as *Self*, in its most basic and true proactive expression of itself as *Spirit* or *I-AM*—free of artificial attachments, perceptive filters and other emotionally-reactive or mentally-conditioned programming imposed on the human condition by the systematized physical world; the ability to experience existence without judgment.

spiritual timeline : a continuous stream of moment-to-moment *Mental Images* (or a record of experiences) that defines the "past" of a spiritual being (or *Alpha-Spirit*) and which includes impressions (*imprints, &tc.*) from all life-incarnations and significant spiritual events the being has encountered; in Systemology, also "*backtrack*."

Spheres of Existence : a series of *eight* concentric circles, rings or spheres (each larger than the former) that is overlaid onto the Standard Model of Beta-Existence to demonstrate the dynamic systems of existence extending out from the POV of Self (often as a "body") at the *First Sphere*; these are given in the basic eightfold systems as: *Self*, *Home/Family*, *Groups*, *Humanity*, *Life on Earth*, *Physical Universe*, *Spiritual Universe* and *Infinity-Divinity*.

Systemology : a modern tradition of applied religious philosophy and spiritual technology based on *Arcane Tablets* (in combination with "*general systemology*" and "*games theory*") developed in the New Age underground by Joshua Free in 2011 as an advanced futurist extension of the *Mardukite Research Org*.

terminal (node) : a point, end, or mass, on a line; a connection point for closing an electric circuit, such as a post on a battery terminating at each end of its own systematic function; a point of connectivity with other points; in systems, a contact point of interaction; a point of interaction with other points.

turbulence : a quality or state of distortion or disturbance that creates irregularity of a flow or pattern; the quality or state of aberration on a line (such as ragged edges) or the emotional "turbulent feelings" attached to a particular flow or terminal node; a violent, haphazard or disharmonious commotion (such as in the ebb of gusts and lulls of wind action).

validation : a reinforcement of agreements or considerations as being "real."

viewpoint : see *"point-of-view" (POV).*

willingness : the state of conscious Self-determined ability and interest (directed attention) to *Be*, *Do* or *Have*; a Self-determined consideration to reach, face up to (*confront*) or manage some "mass" or energy; the extent to which an individual considers themselves able to participate, act or communicate along some line, to put attention or intention on the line, or to produce (create) an effect.

ZU : the ancient Sumerian cuneiform sign for the archaic verb—*"to know,"* *"knowingness"* or *"awareness"*; in *Mardukite Zuism and Systemology*, the active energy/matter of the "Spiritual Universe" (AN) experienced as a *Lifeforce* or *consciousness* that imbues living forms extant in the "Physical Universe" (KI); *"Spiritual Life Energy"*; energy demonstrated by the WILL of an actualized *Alpha-Spirit* in the "Spiritual Universe" (AN), which impinges its *Awareness* into the Physical Universe (KI), animating/controlling *Life* for its experience of *beta-existence* along an individual Alpha-Spirit's personal *Identity-continuum*, called a *ZU-line*.

***Zu*-Line** : a theoretical construct in *Mardukite Zuism and Systemology* demonstrating *Spiritual*

Life Energy (*ZU*) as a personal individual "continuum" of Awareness interacting with all Spheres of Existence on the Standard Model of Systemology; a spectrum of potential variations and interactions of a monistic continuum or singular *Spiritual Life Energy* demonstrated on the Standard Model; an energetic channel of potential POV and "locations" of Beingness, demonstrated in early Systemology materials as an individual Alpha-Spirit's personal *Identity- continuum*, potentially connecting *Awareness* of *Self* with "*Infinity*" simultaneous with all points considered in existence; a symbolic demonstration of the "*Life-line*" on which *Awareness (ZU)* extends from the direction of the "Spiritual Universe" (AN) in its true original *alpha state* through an entire possible range of activity resulting in its *beta state* and control of a *genetic-entity* occupying the *Physical Universe (KI)*.

***Zu*-Vision** : the true and basic (*Alpha*) Point-of-View (perspective, POV) maintained by *Self* as *Alpha-Spirit* outside boundaries or considerations of the *Human Condition* and *exterior* to beta-existence reality agreements with the Physical Universe; a POV of Self *as* "a unit of Spiritual Awareness" that exists independent of a "body" and entrapment in a *Human Condition*; "spirit vision" in its truest sense.

AVAILABLE FROM THE **JOSHUA FREE** PUBLISHING IMPRINT

Collector's Edition Hardcover

THE FUNDAMENTALS OF

SYSTEMOLOGY

A Basic Course developed by
Joshua Free

collecting material of six lesson-booklets together in one volume!

"Being More Than Human"

"Realities in Agreement"

"Windows To Experience"

"Ancient Systemology"

"A History of Systemology"

"Systemology Processing"

All *six* lesson-booklets of the first official *Basic Course* on Mardukite Systemology are combined together in *one volume* as *"Fundamentals of Systemology."*

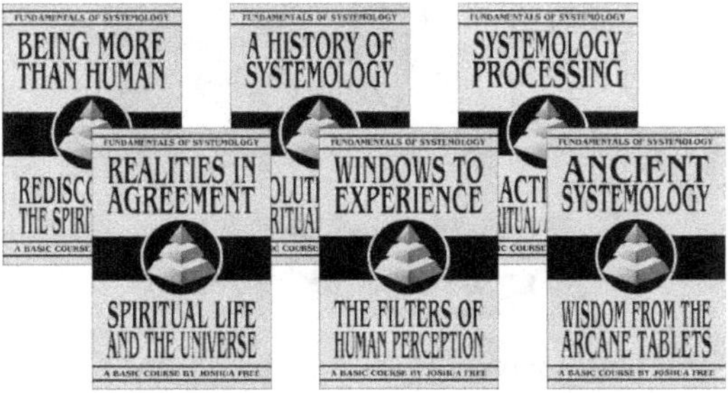

Lesson booklets are also available individually!

AVAILABLE FROM THE **JOSHUA FREE** PUBLISHING IMPRINT

Collector's Edition Hardcover

THE PATHWAY TO

ASCENSION

The Official 2024 Systemology
Professional Course by
Joshua Free

All sixteen lessons available in two volumes!

"Increasing Awareness"

"Thought & Emotion"

"Clear Communication"

"Handling Humanity"

"Free Your Spirit"

"Escaping Spirit-Traps"

"Eliminating Barriers"

"Conquest of Illusion"

All *sixteen* lesson-booklets of the newest *Professional Course* on Mardukite Systemology are combined together in *two volumes* as "*The Pathway to Ascension.*"

Lesson booklets are also available individually!

"The Secret of Universes"

"Games, Goals and Purposes"

"The Jewel of Knowledge"

"Implanted Universes"

"Entities and Fragments"

"Spiritual Perception"

"Mastering Ascension"

"Advancing Systemology"

All *eight* A.T. manuals of the *New Standard* Systemology *Advanced Training Course* along with *three* training supplements are combined together in *two volumes* as *"Keys to the Kingdom."*

Manuals are also available as individual booklets!

THE SYSTEM

Seekers and students of the *Professional Course* and *Advanced Training Course* will also be interested in the original *Systemology Core Research Series.* These *8* volumes are a complete chronological record of *Mardukite NexGen New Thought* developments published by the *Systemology Society* from 2019 through 2023.

The Systemology Core series begins with the first professional publication released when our *Mardukite Systemology* emerged from the underground in 2019, with: *"The Tablets of Destiny Revelation."*

OLOGY CORE

The Tablets of Destiny Revelation:
How Long-Lost Anunnaki Wisdom
Can Change the Fate of Humanity

Crystal Clear: *Handbook for Seekers*

Metahuman Destinations (*2 volumes*)

Imaginomicon:
Approaching Gateways to Higher Universes

Way of the Wizard: *Utilitarian Systemology*

Systemology-180: *Fast-Track to Ascension*

Systemology Backtrack:
Reclaiming Spiritual Power & Past-Life Memory

PUBLISHED BY THE **JOSHUA FREE** IMPRINT REPRESENTING

The Mardukite Academy of Systemology

THE JOSHUA FREE IMPRINT
JFI PUBLICATIONS

MARDUKITE
ZUISM

mardukite.com

www.ingramcontent.com/pod-product-compliance
Lightning Source LLC
Chambersburg PA
CBHW061145120626
46546CB00005B/1930
* 9 7 8 1 9 6 1 5 0 9 5 4 2 *